Rainer Strzolka

The Workshop

Pictures from the German misery

Hannover Berlin Straßberg

Galerie für Kulturkommunikation

2024

This exhibition catalog shows pictures of German misery.

The workshop was once the epitome of high-quality craftsmanship. Those days are long gone. Today, "workshop" is the opposite of what it once meant.

Today, "workshop" is the term for a horde of knitting, purring, discussing social workers whose only purpose in life is the so-called "social question" and who see every drug addict as a victim of the evil, evil society.

While the workshop used to be the driving force of social prosperity, it has become the opposite: a chatterbox without any social, economic or moral benefit.

This exhibition catalog shows the rotten remains of a classic workshop as it will never exist again.

All the pictures shown here were shown as analog prints in this very workshop one month after they were taken and given away to visitors after exactly one day.

Please also visit us on the Internet. We look forward to your visit.

www.galerie-fuer-kulturkommunikation.de

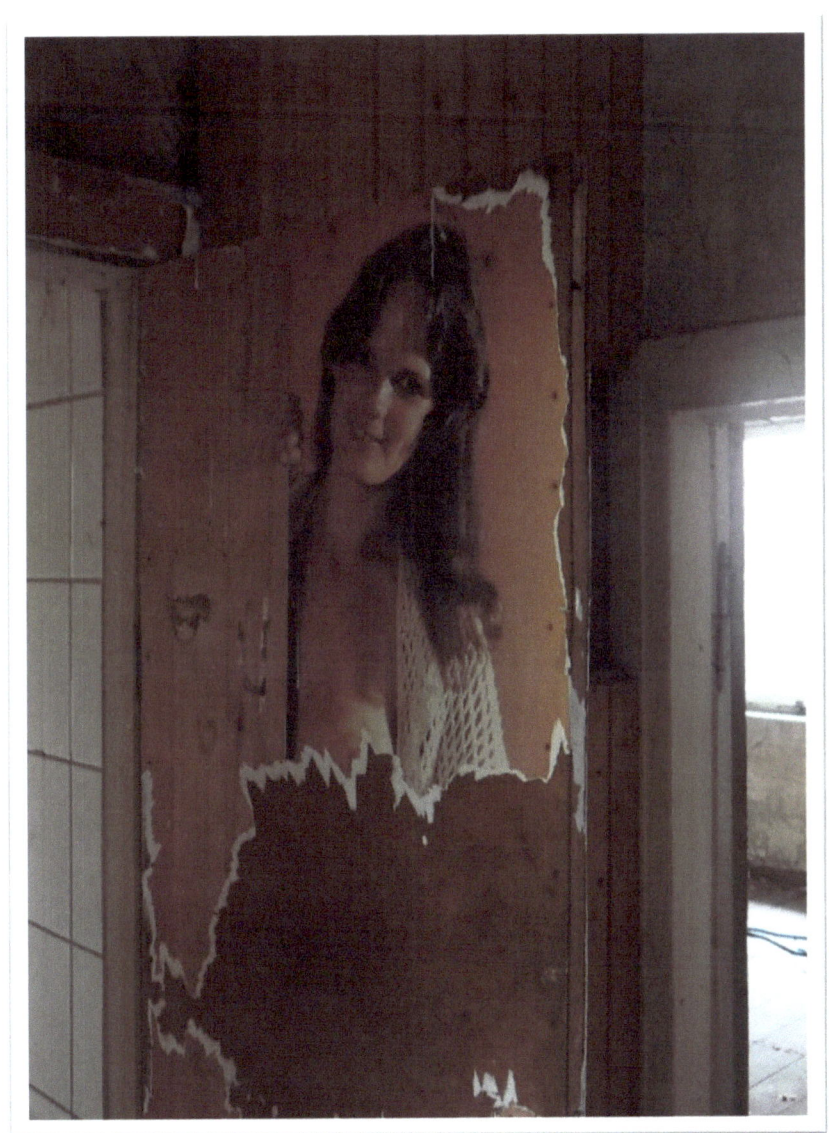

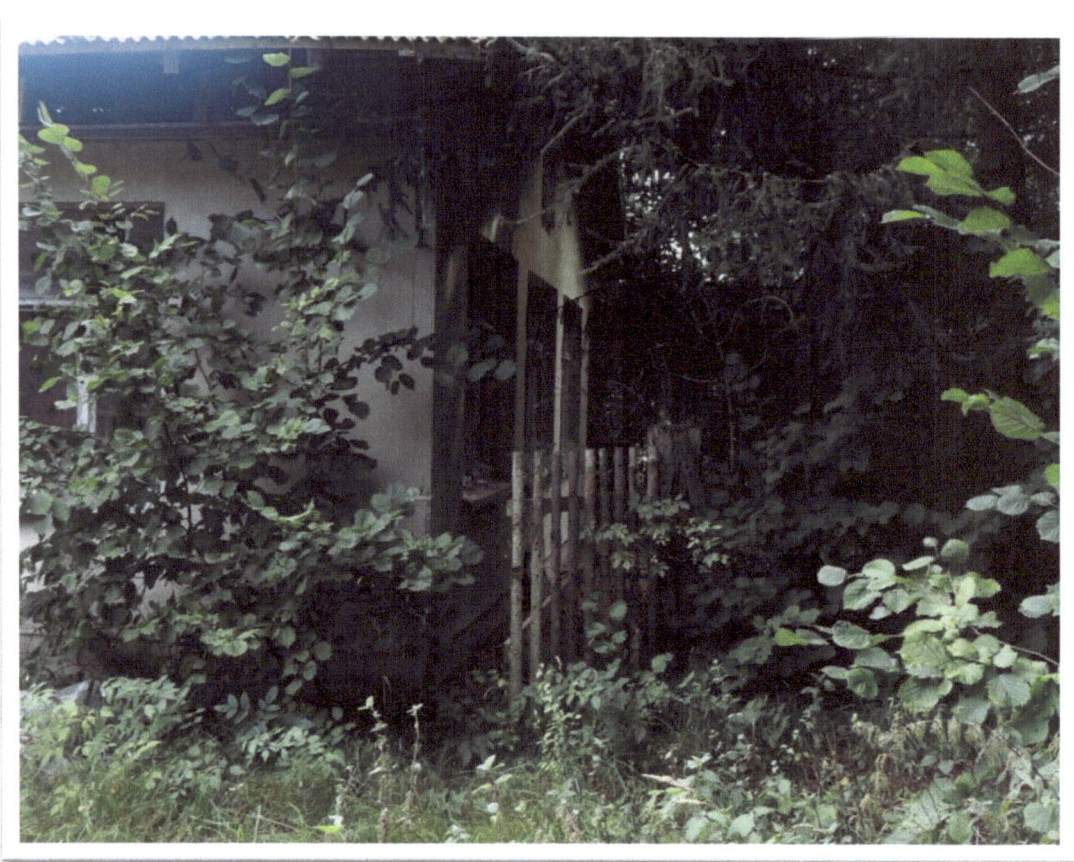

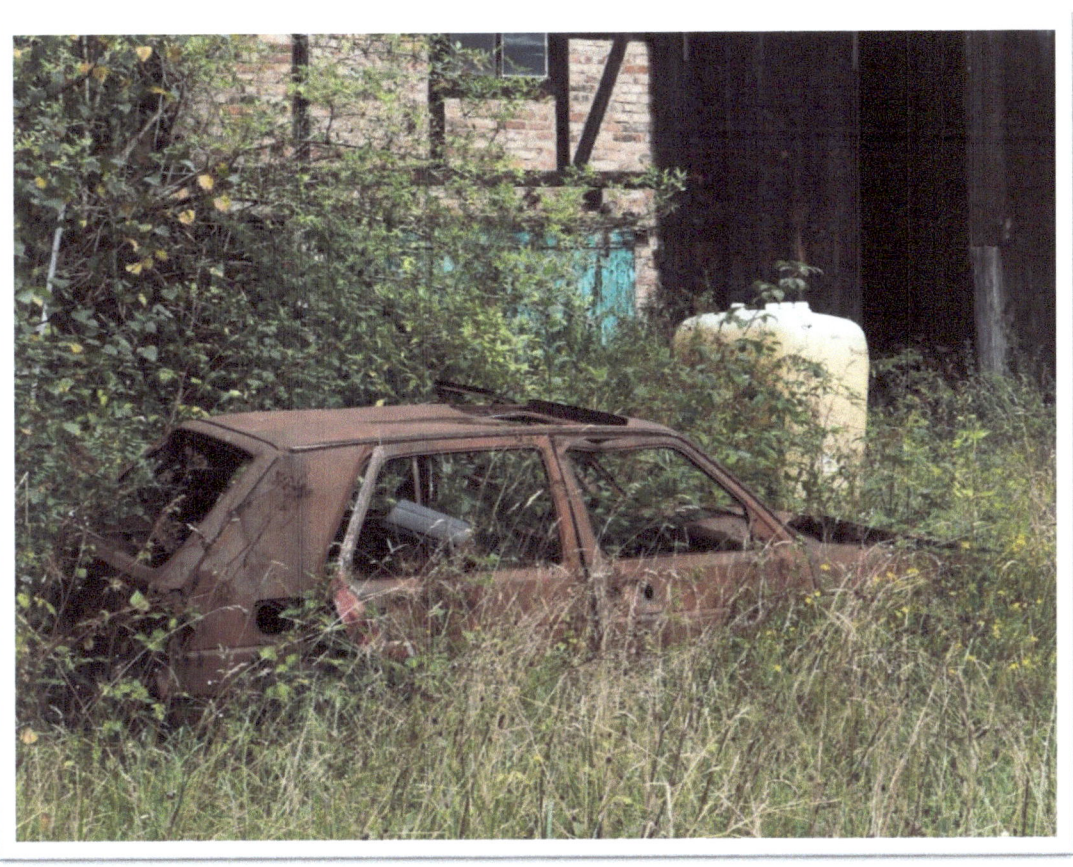

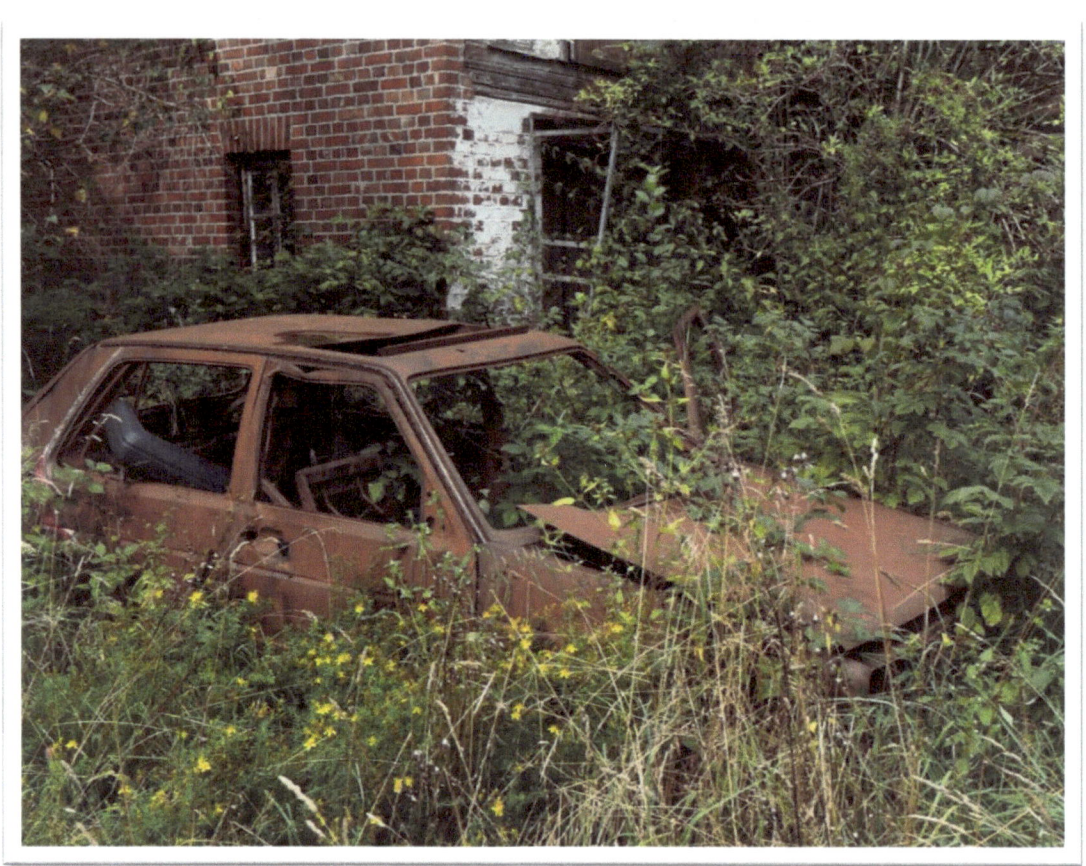

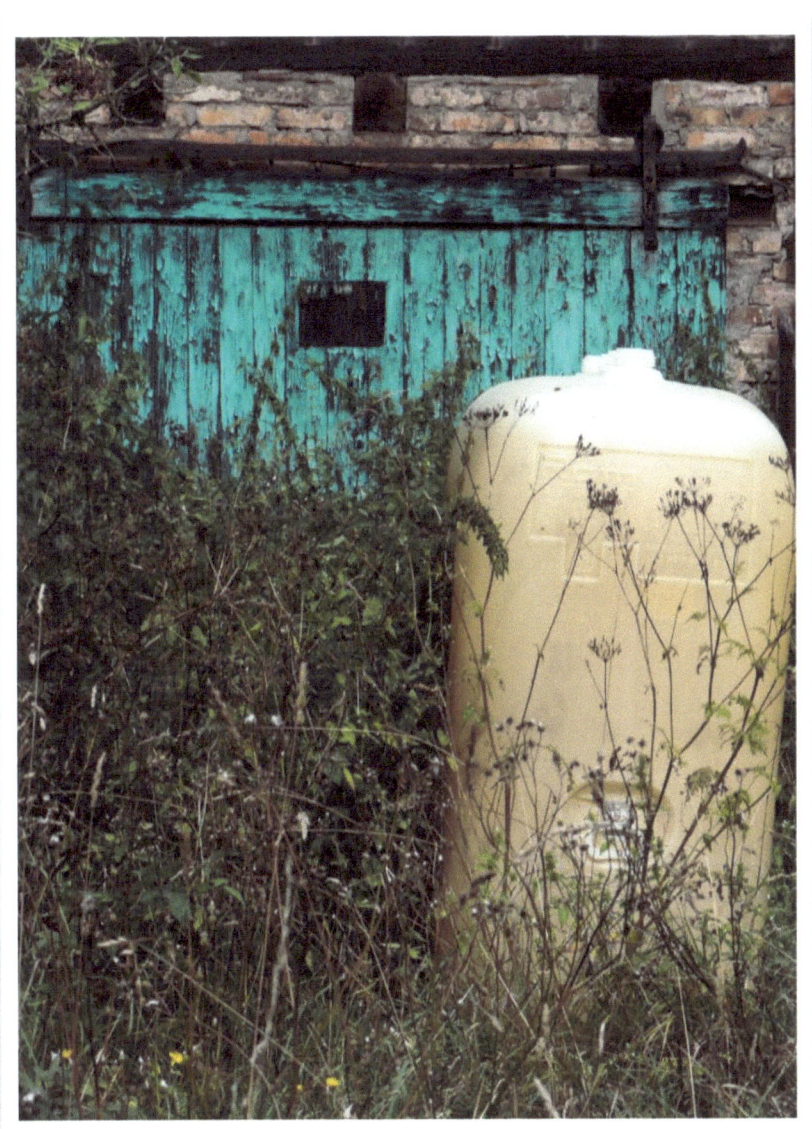

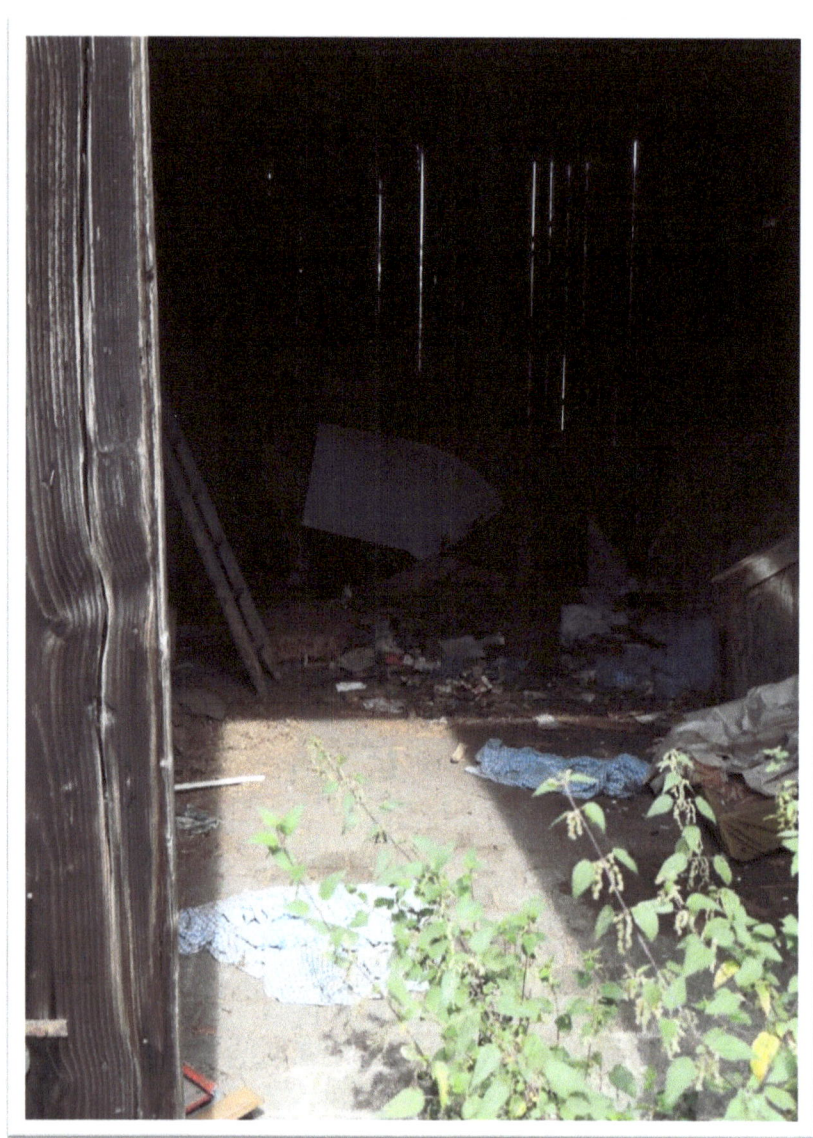

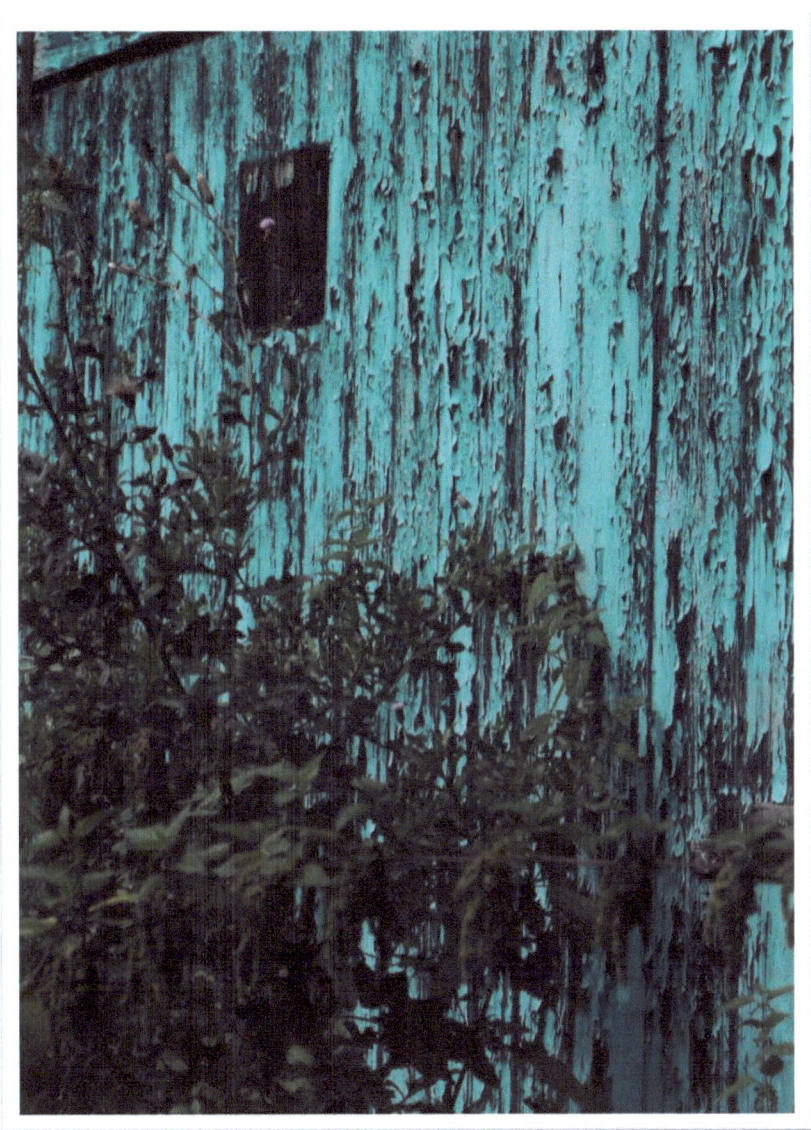

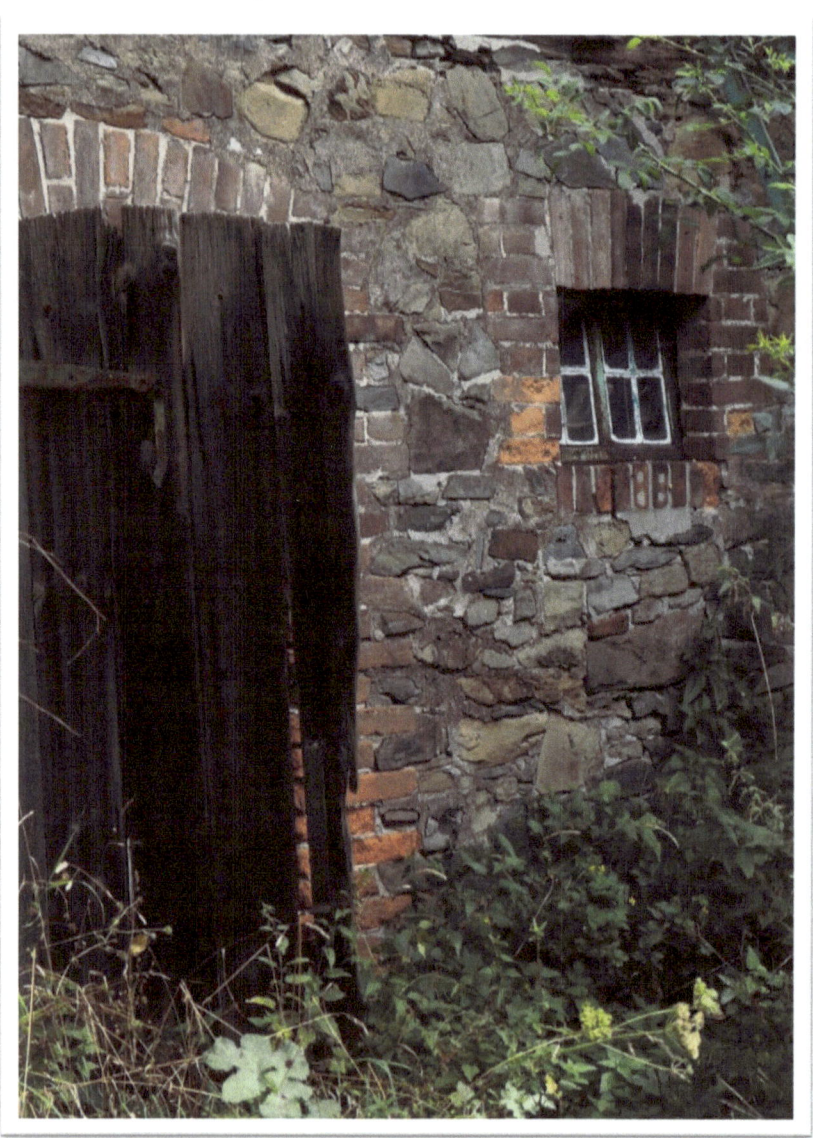

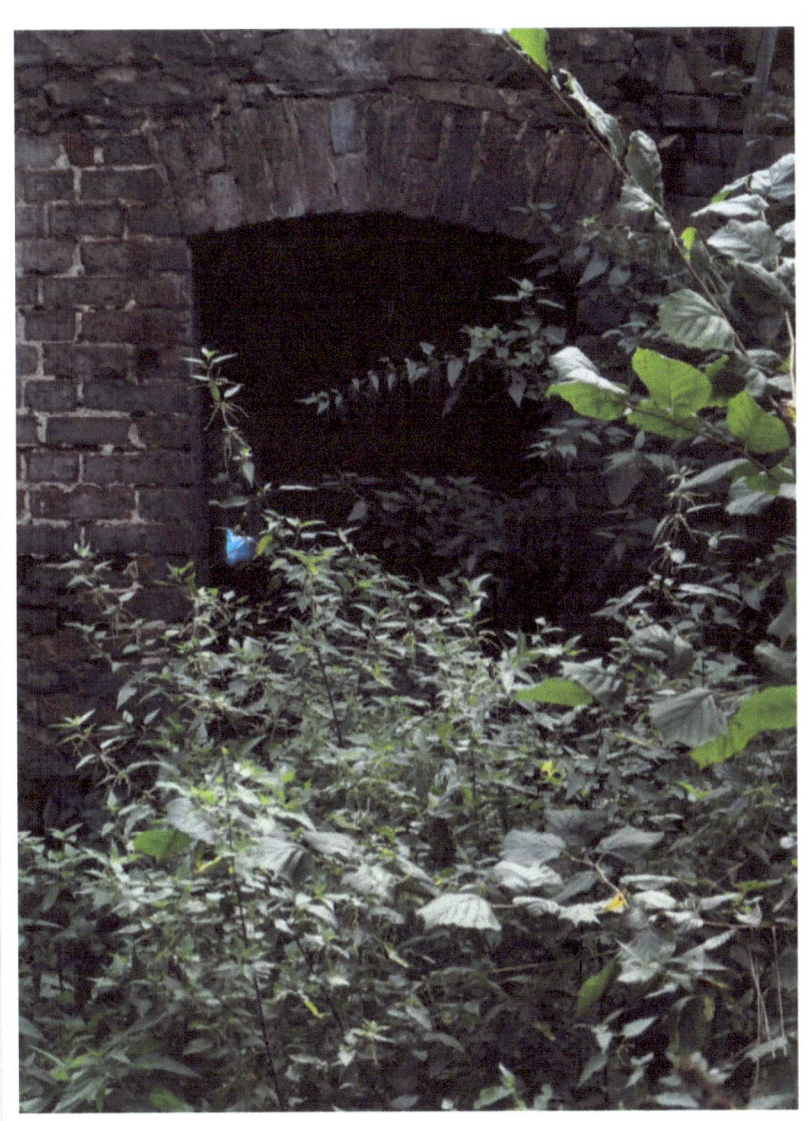

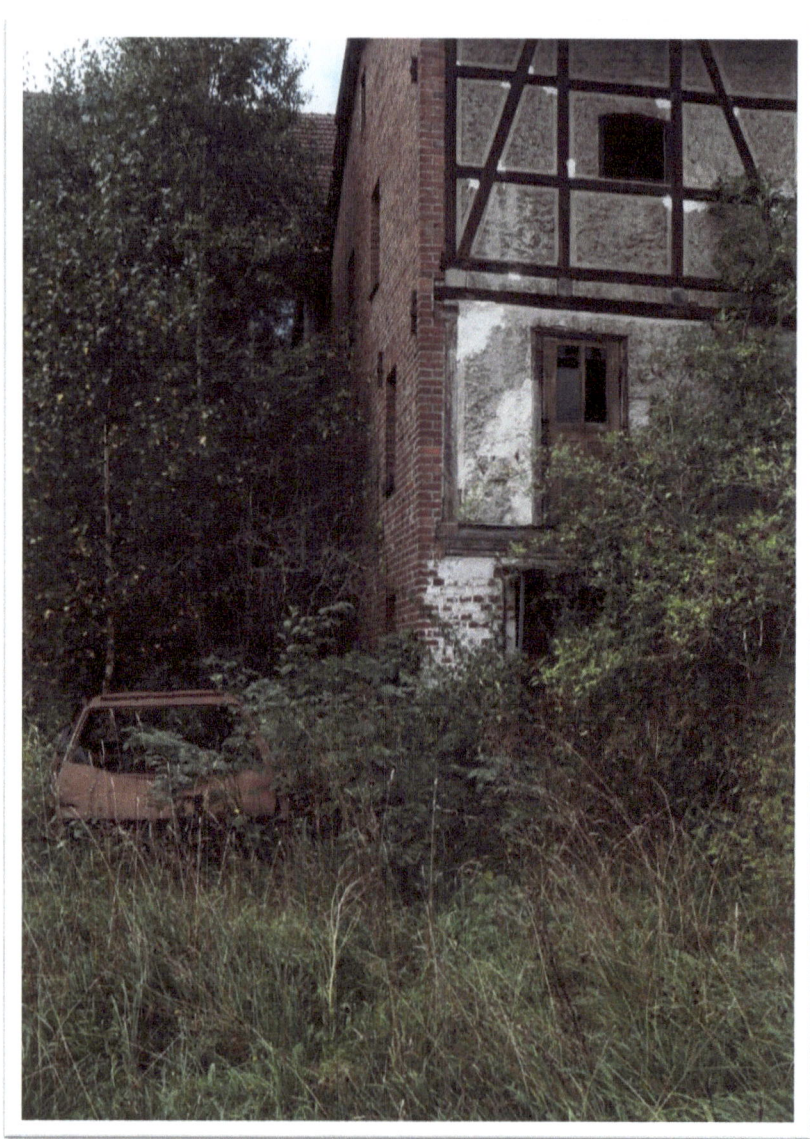

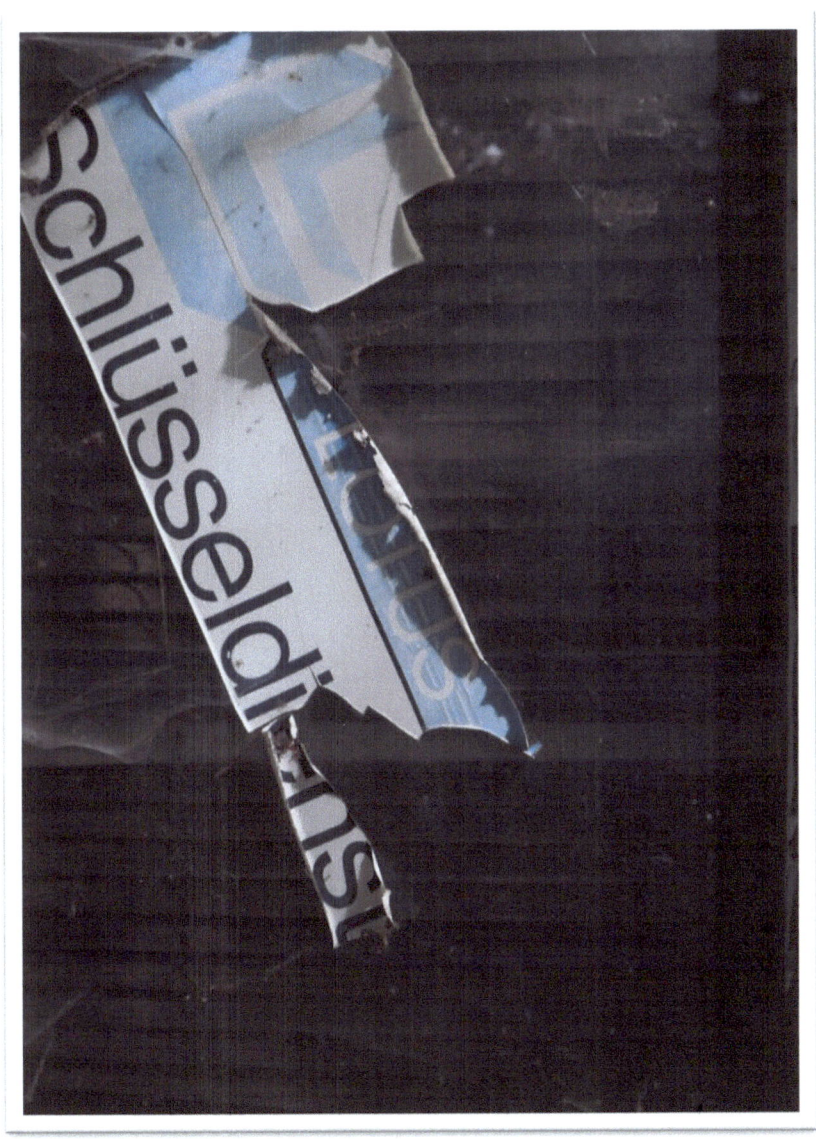

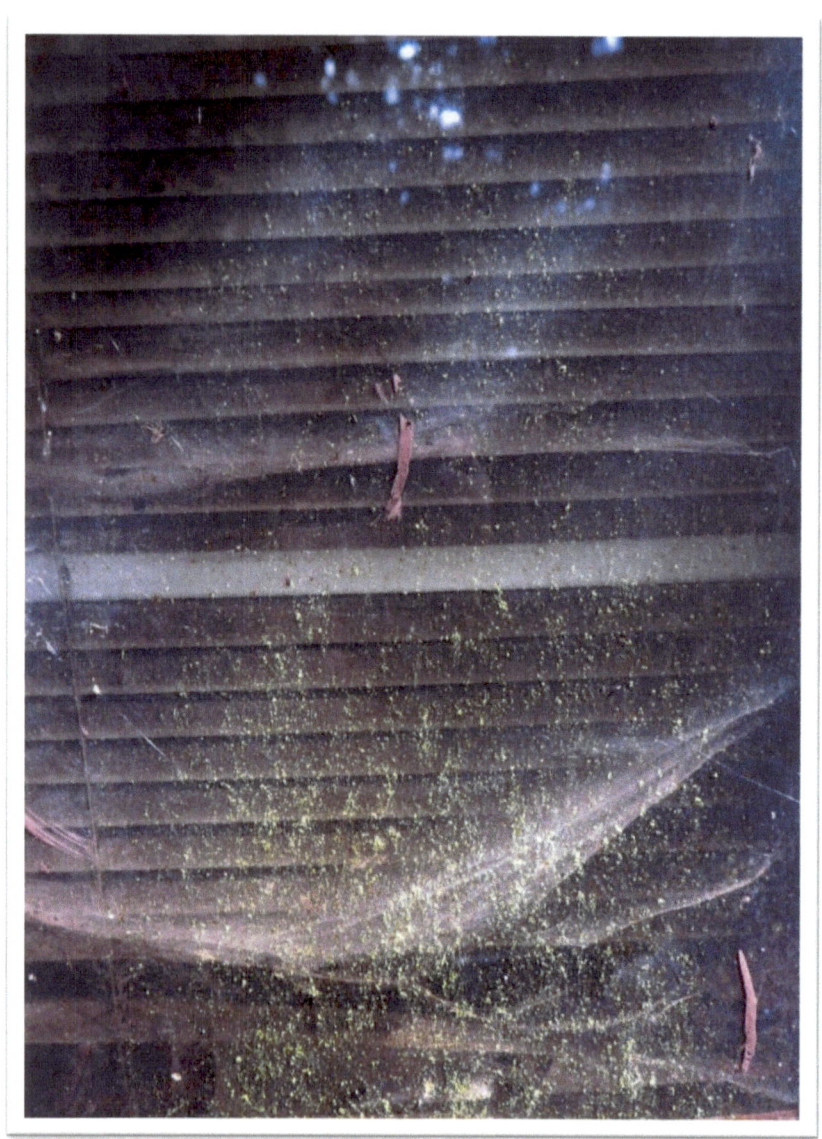

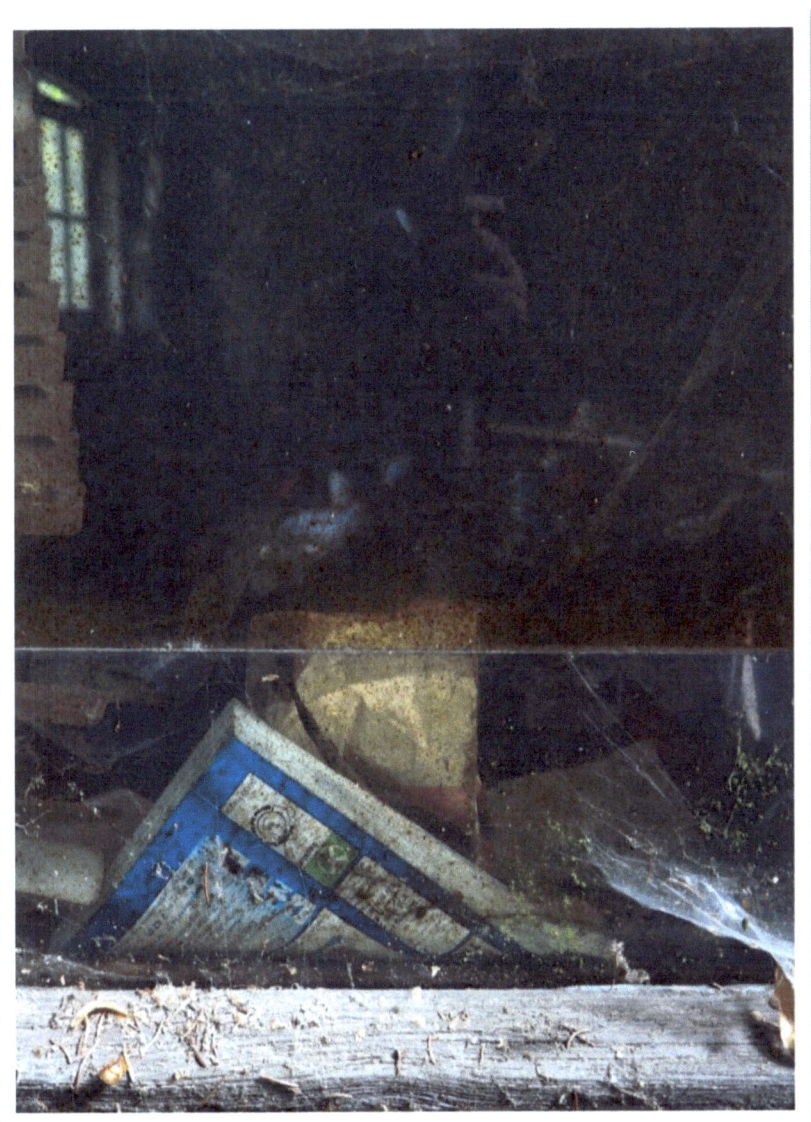

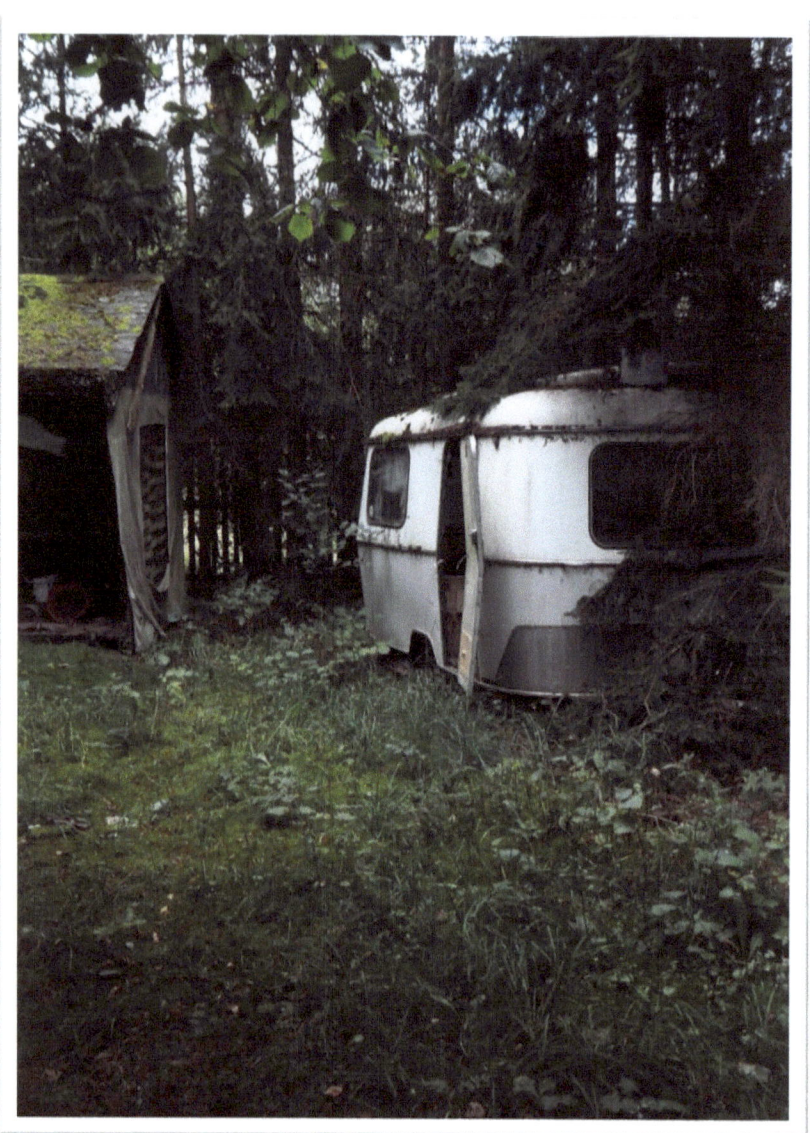

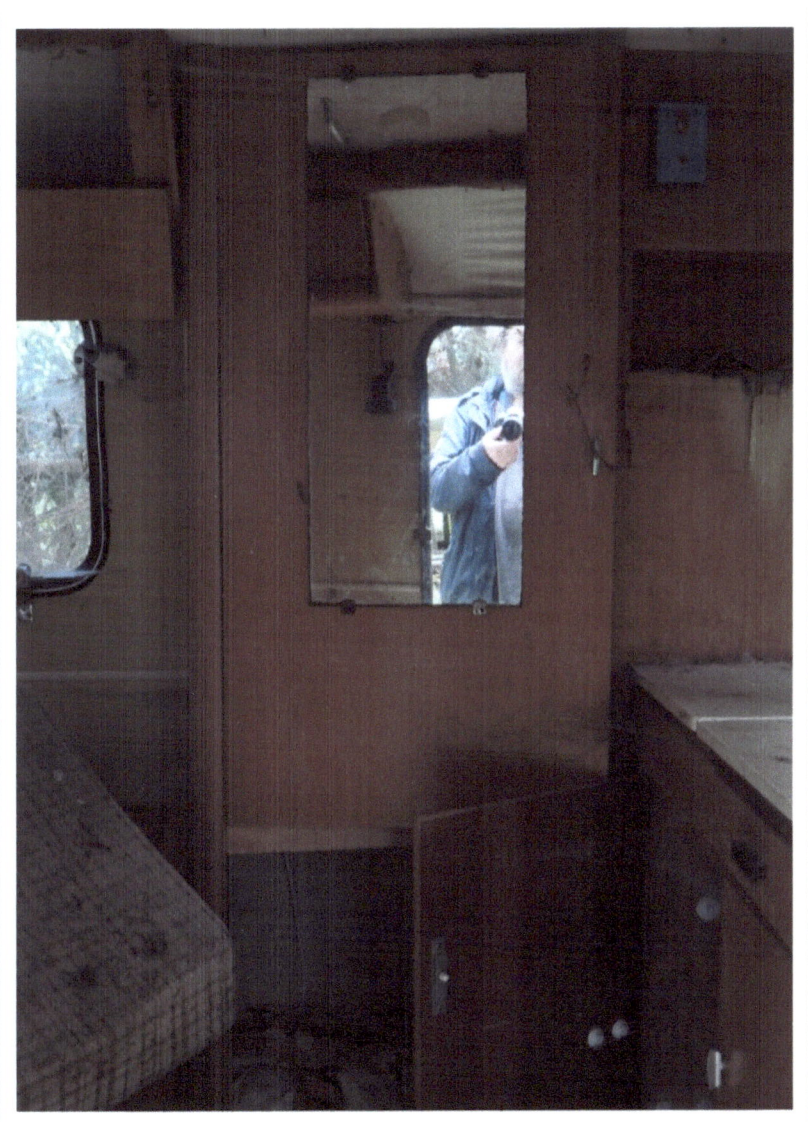

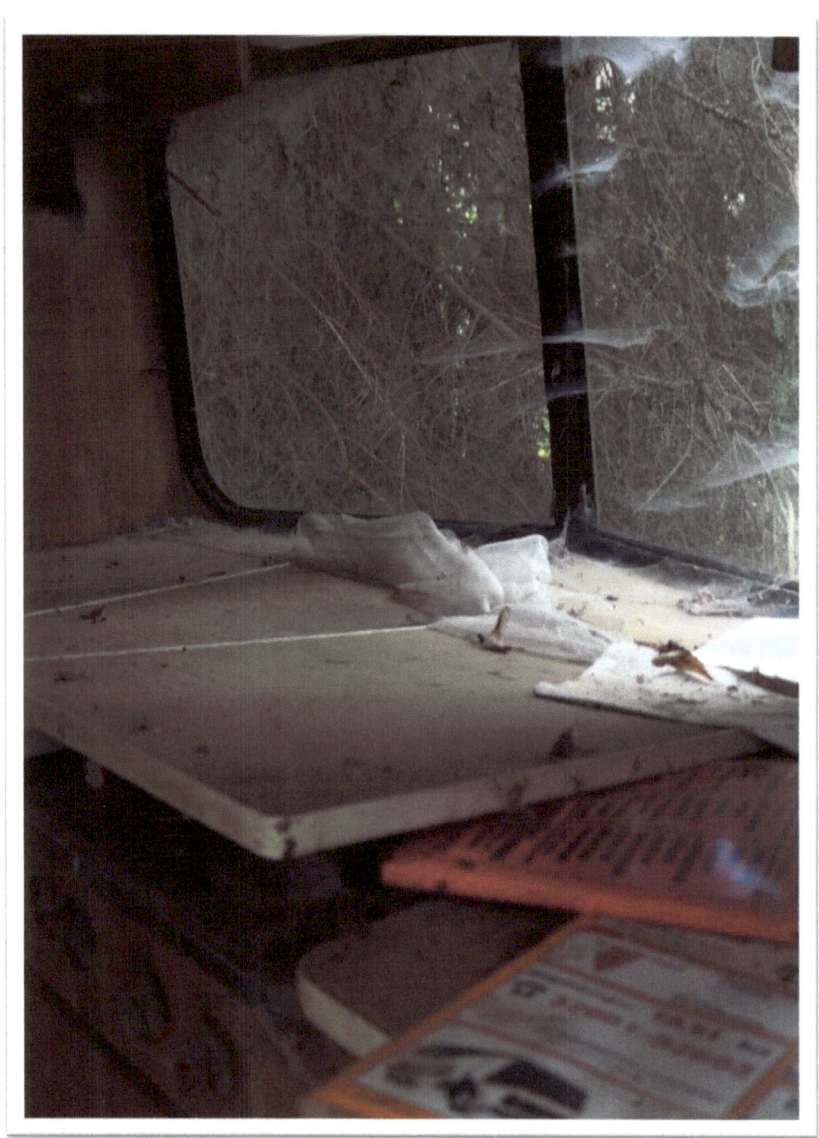

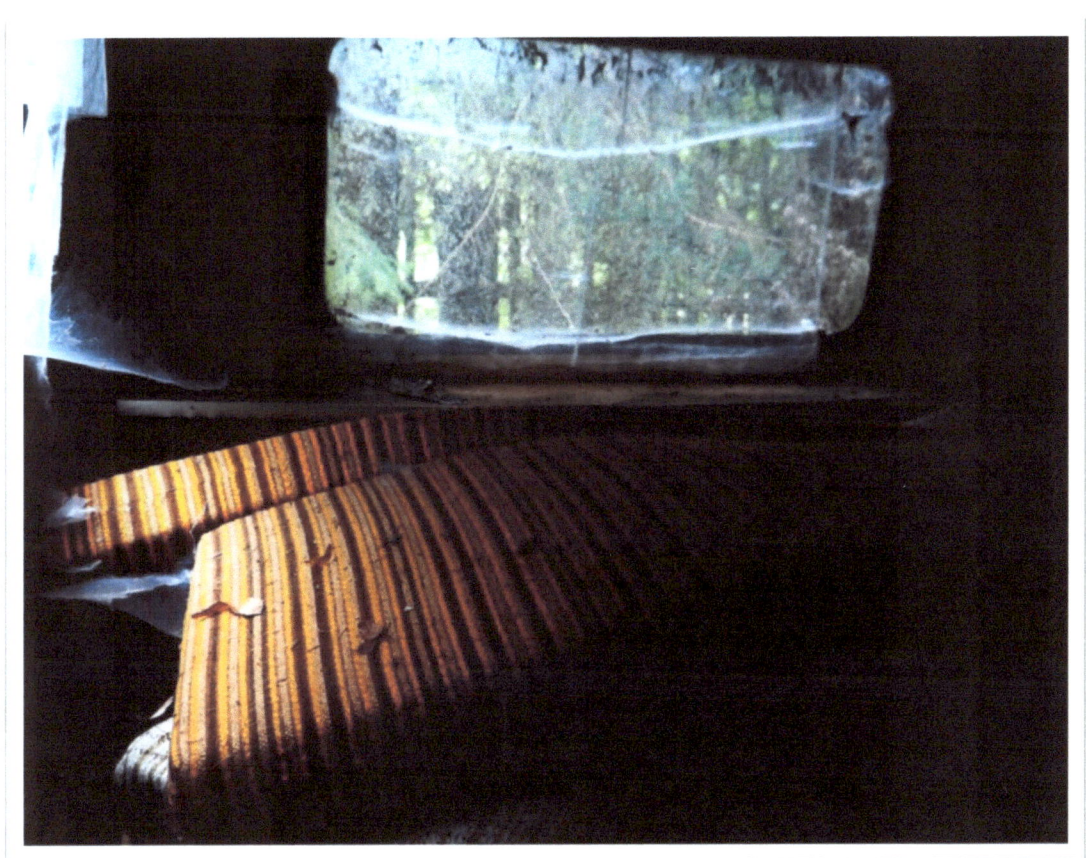

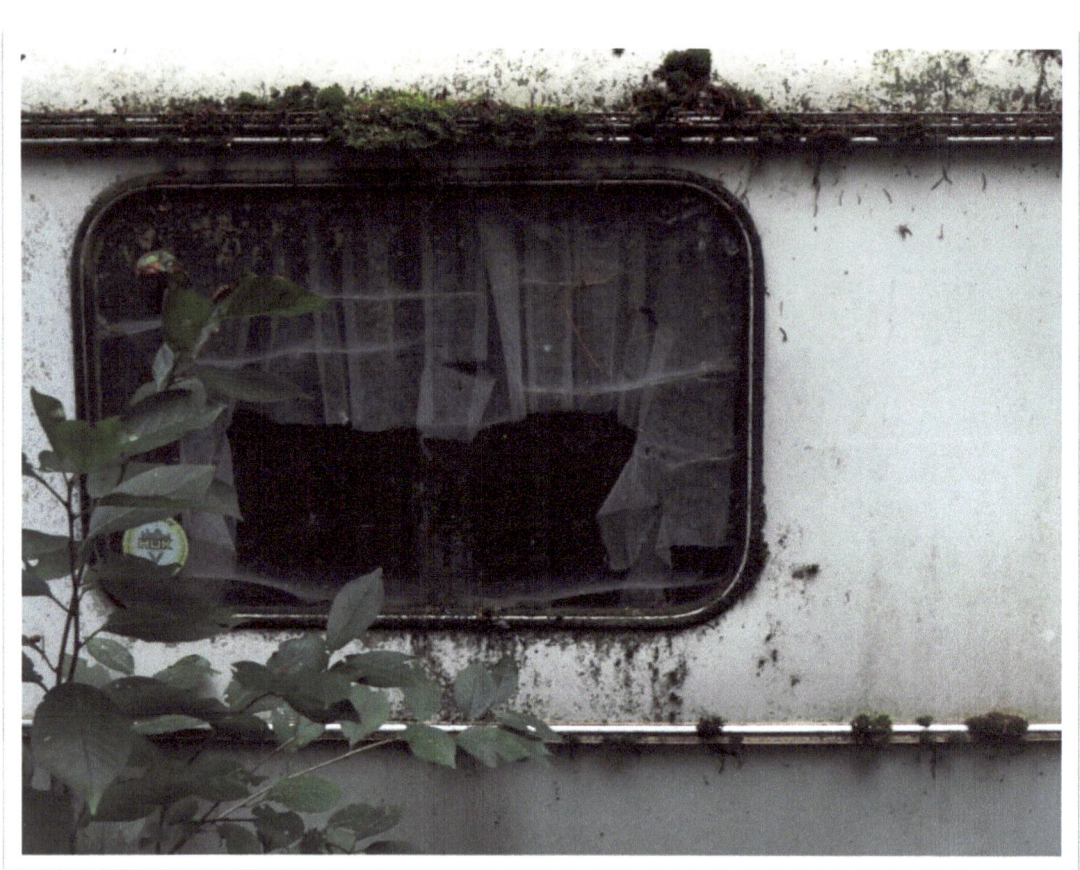

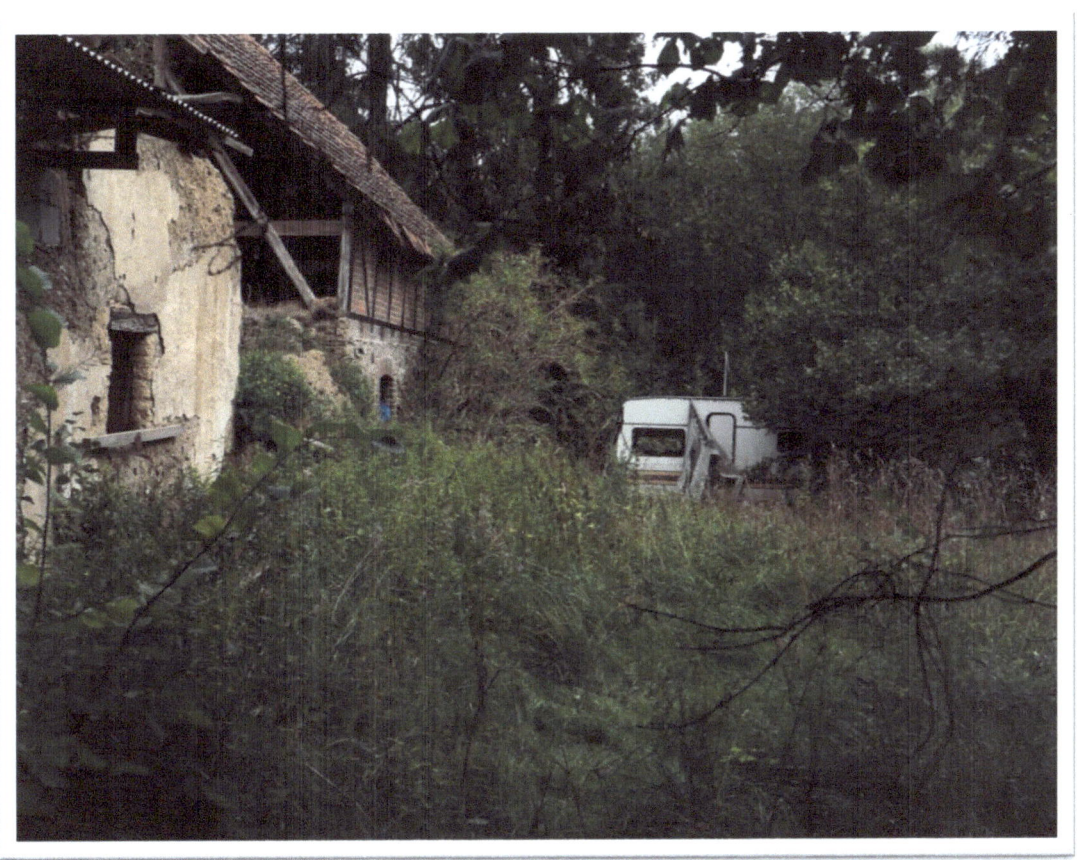

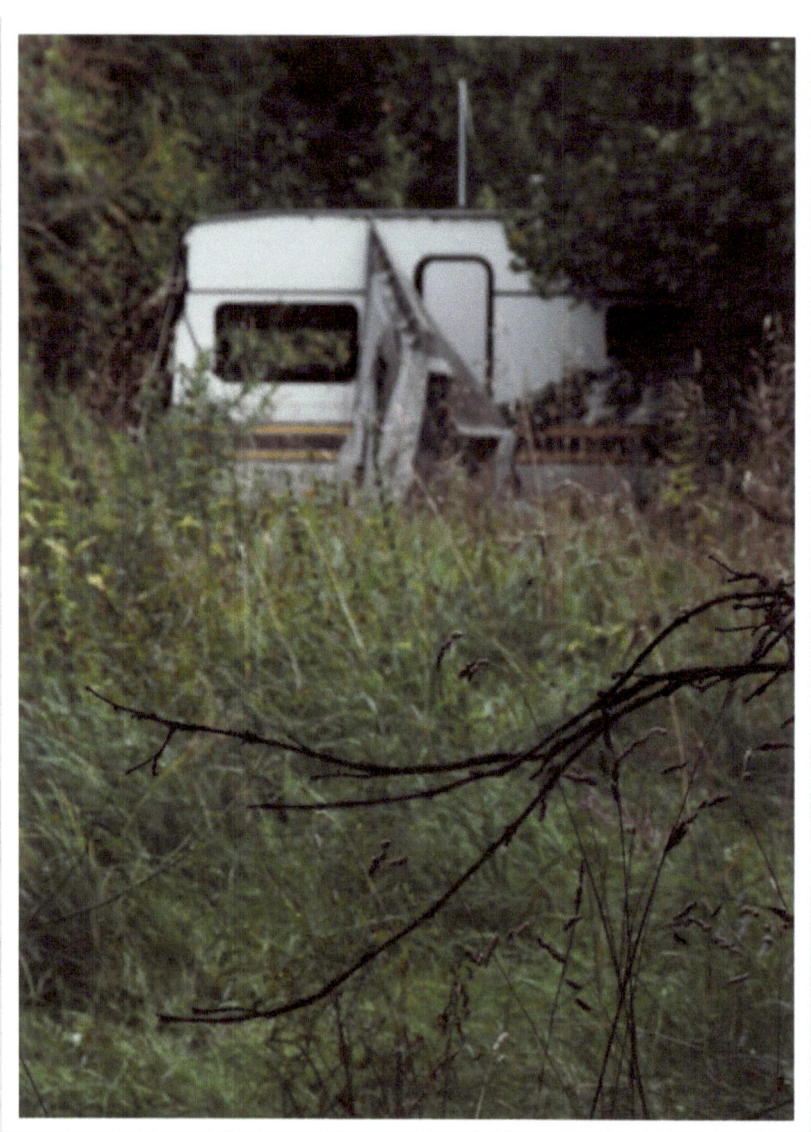

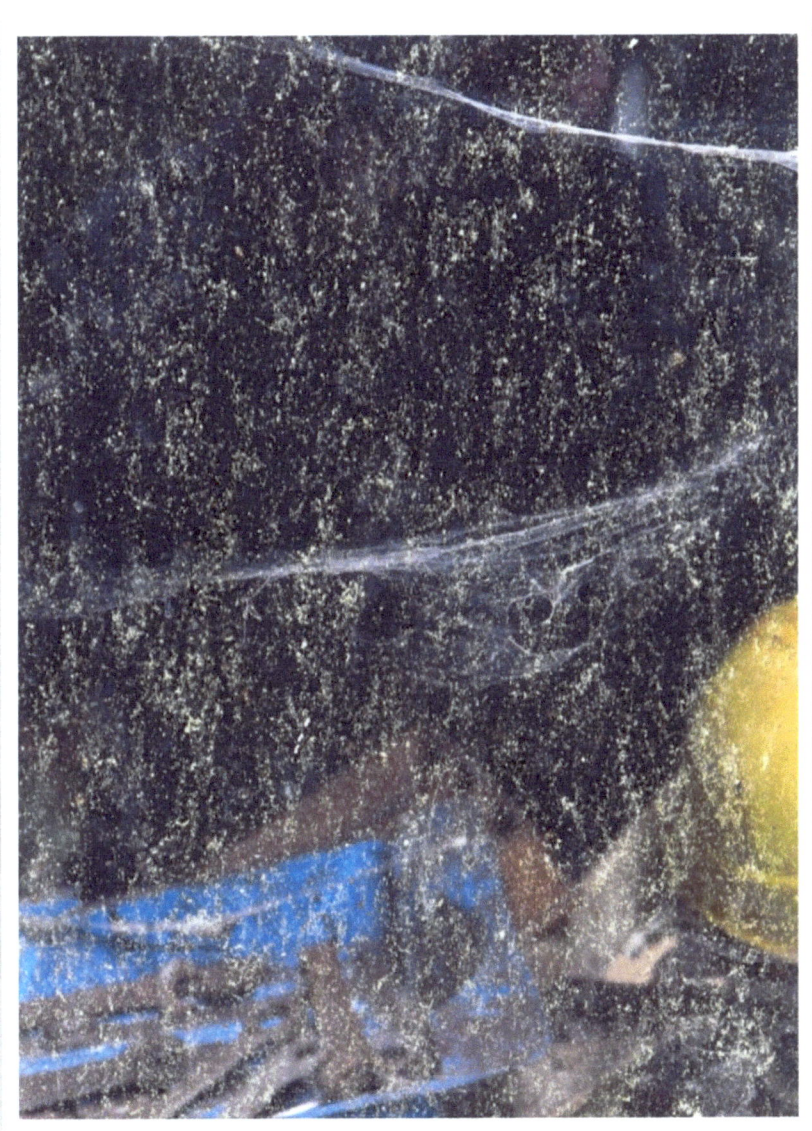

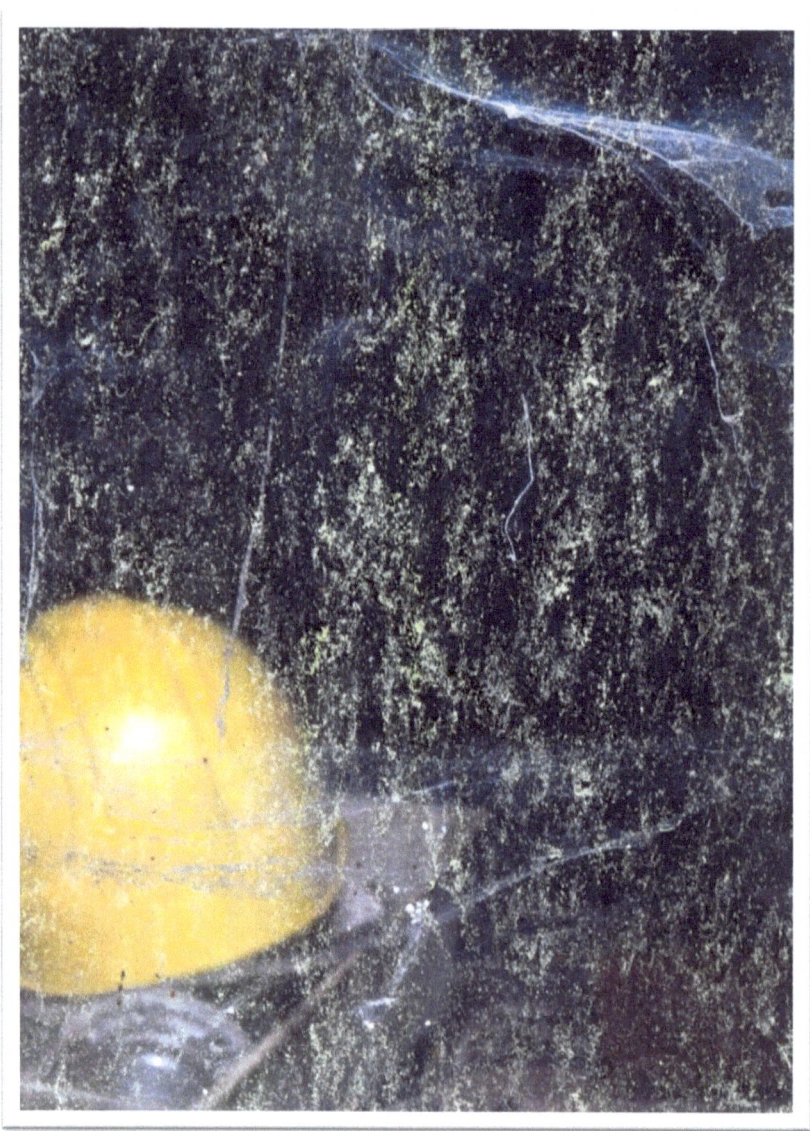

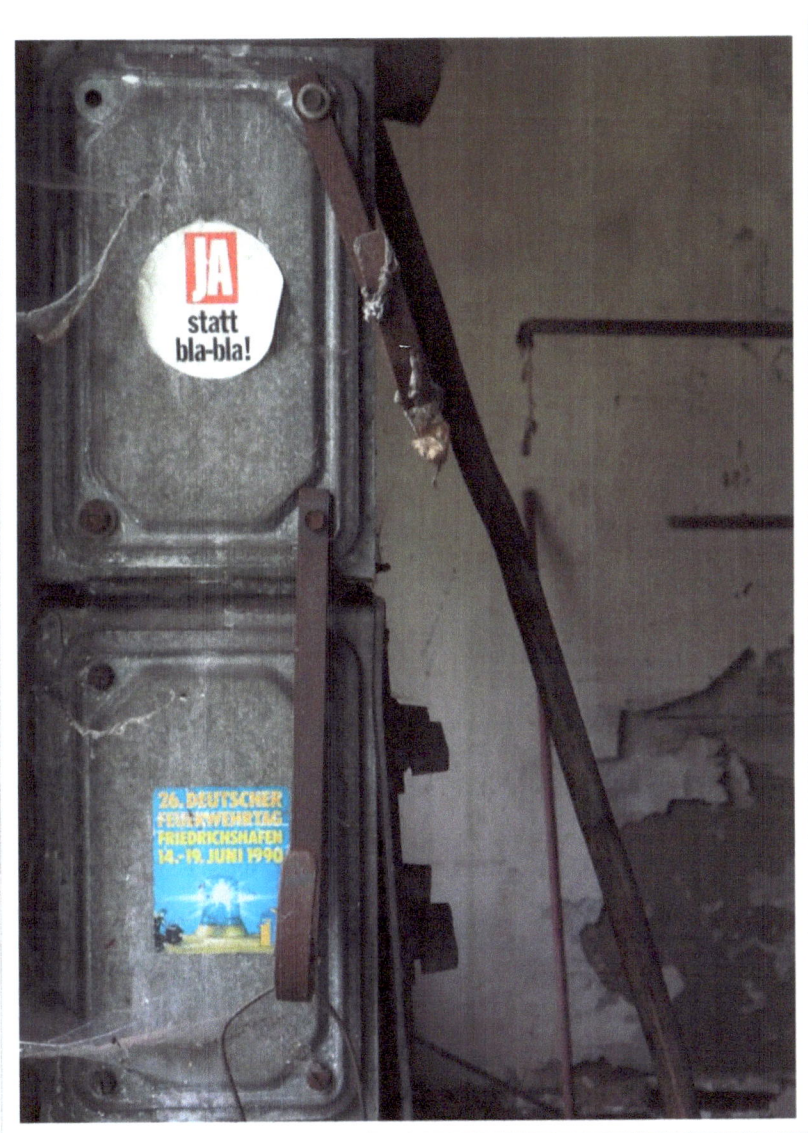

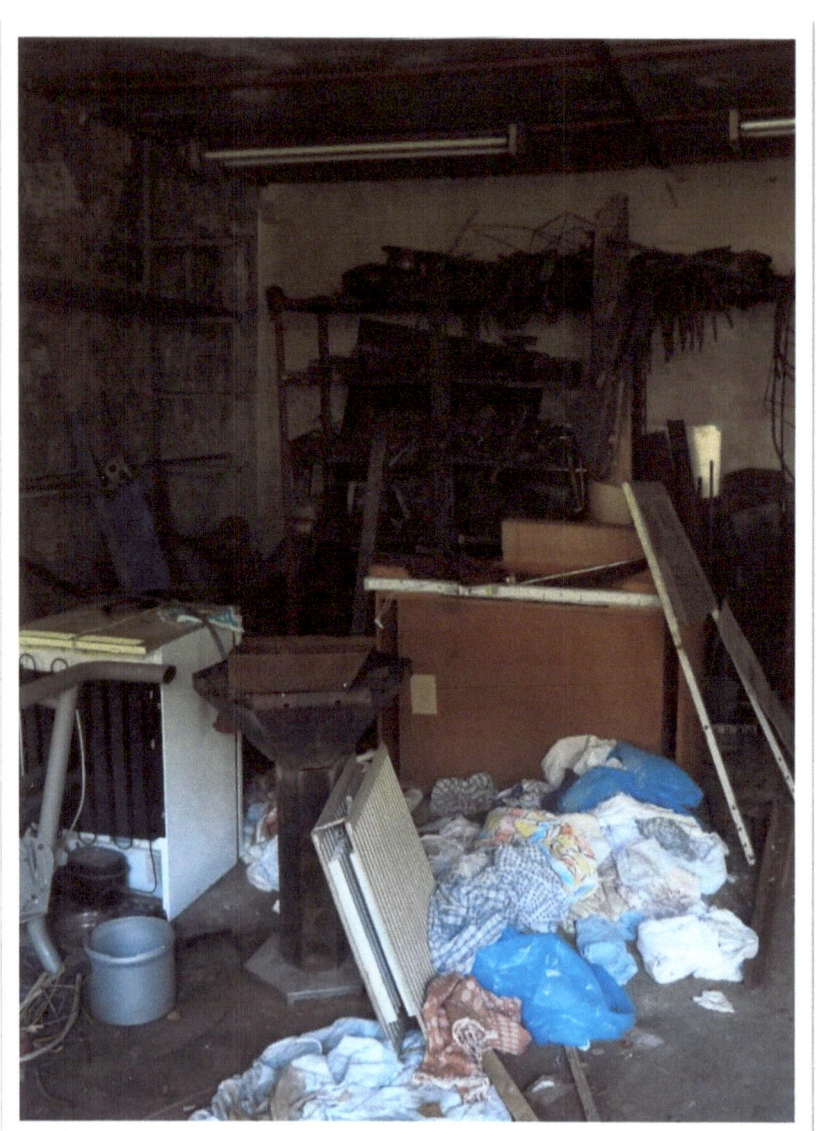

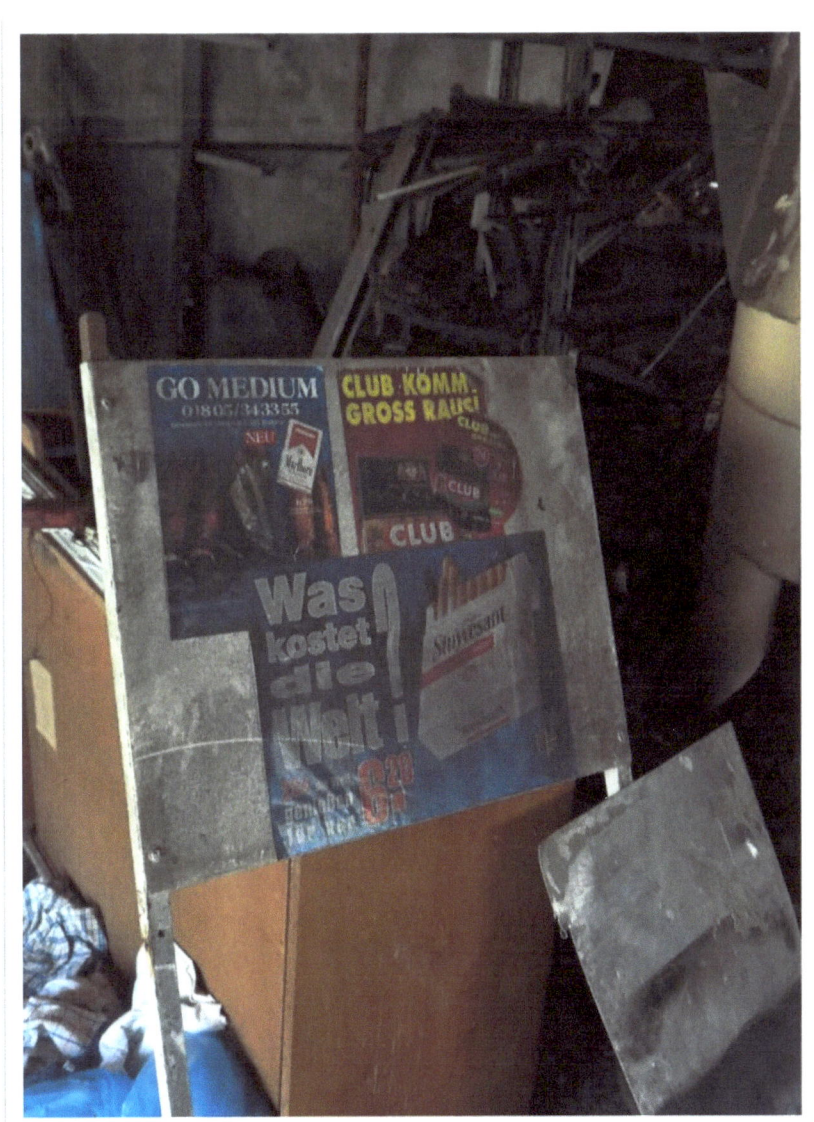

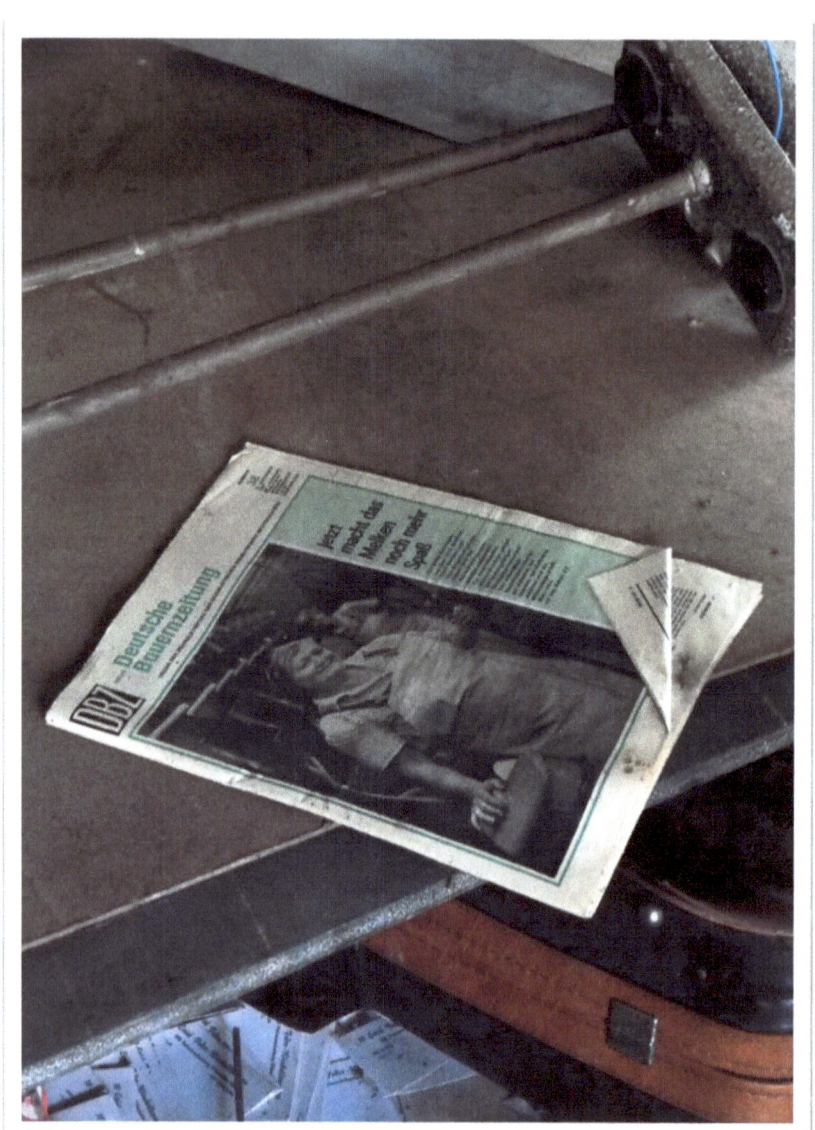

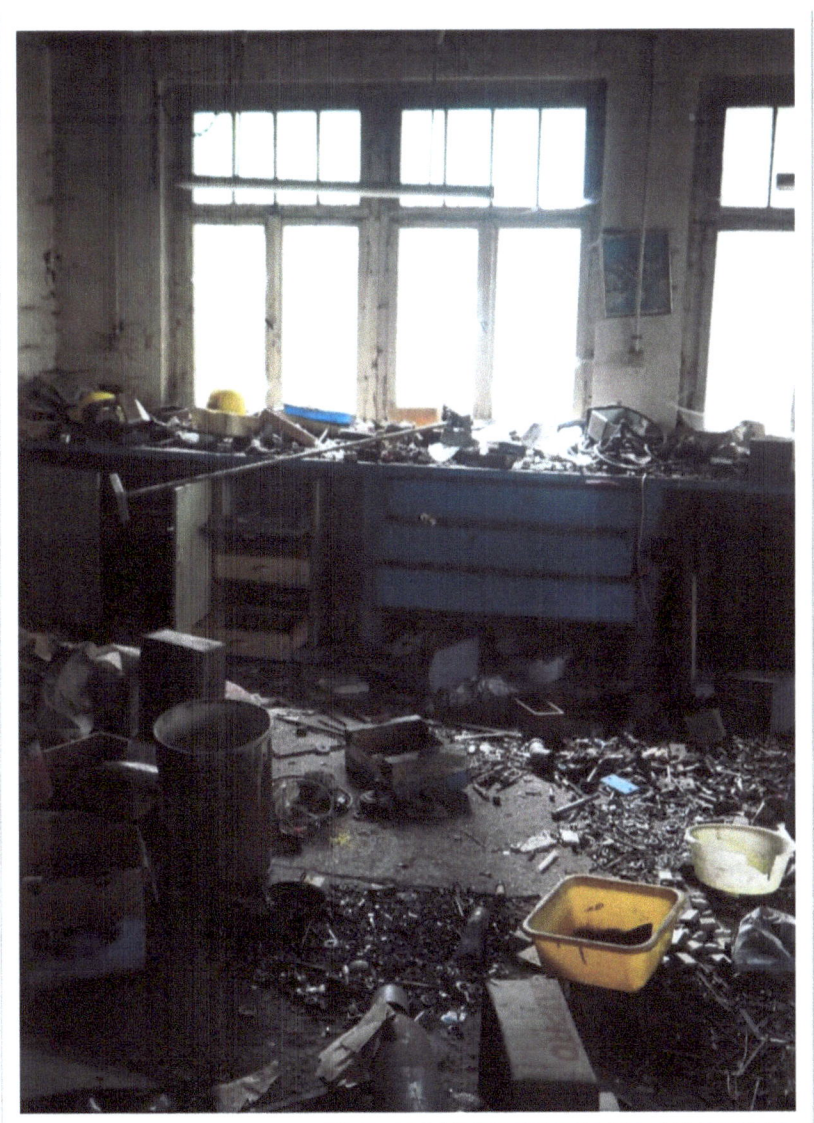

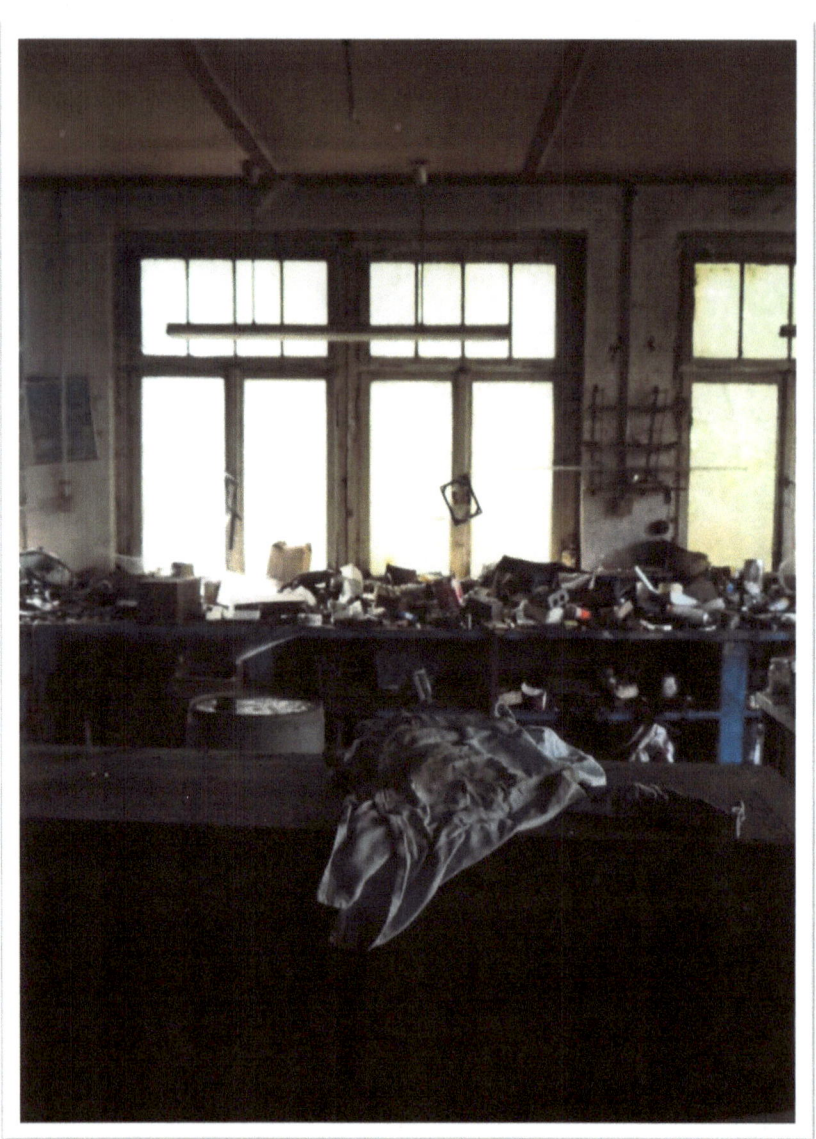

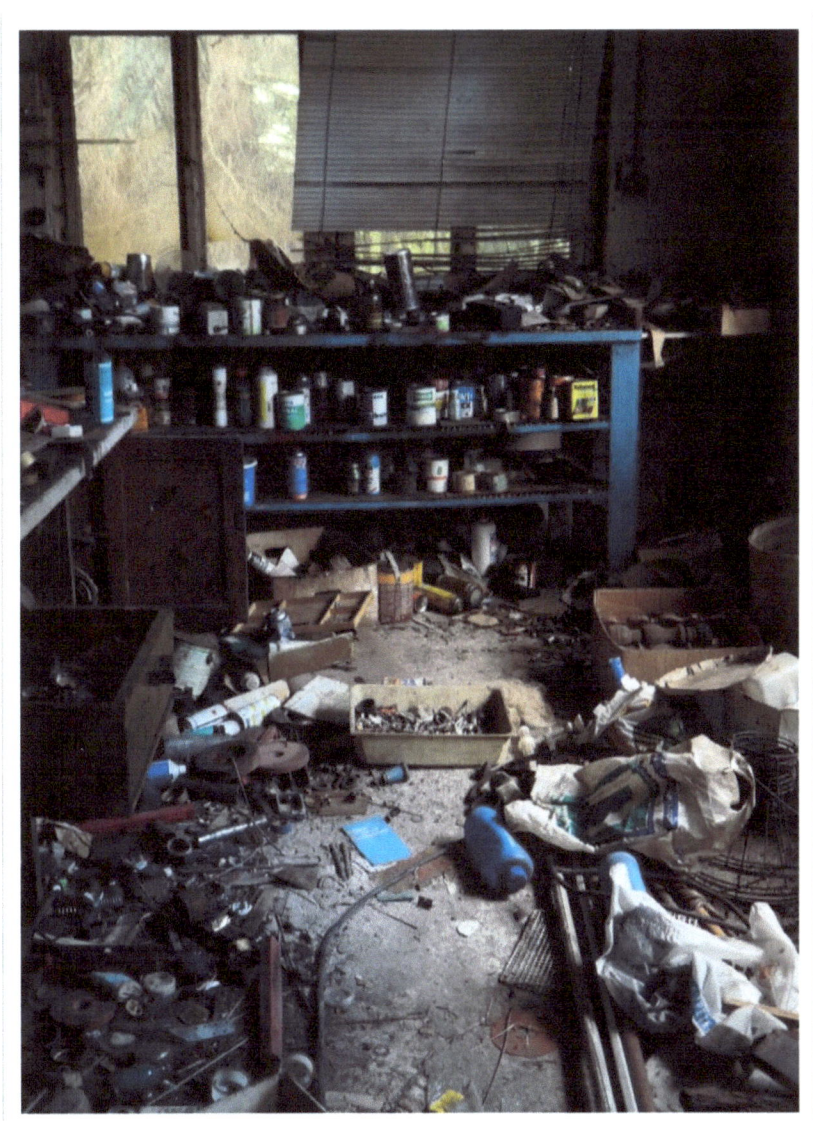

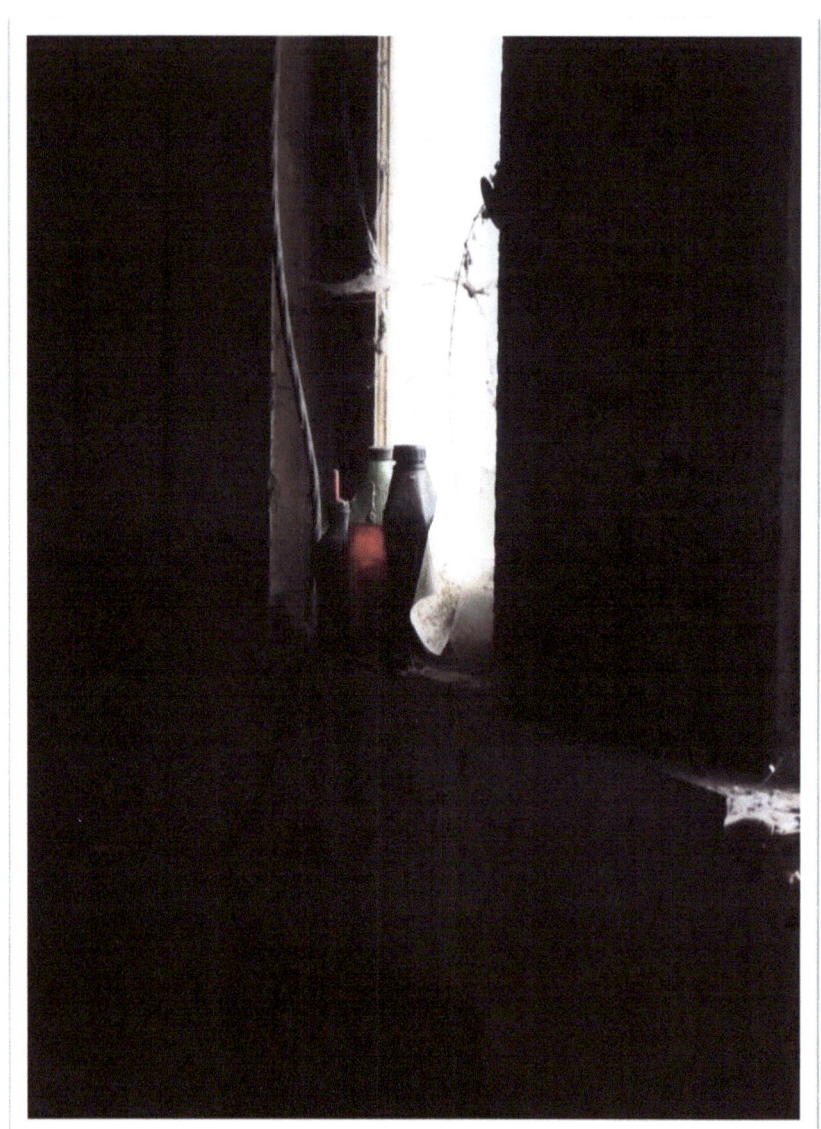

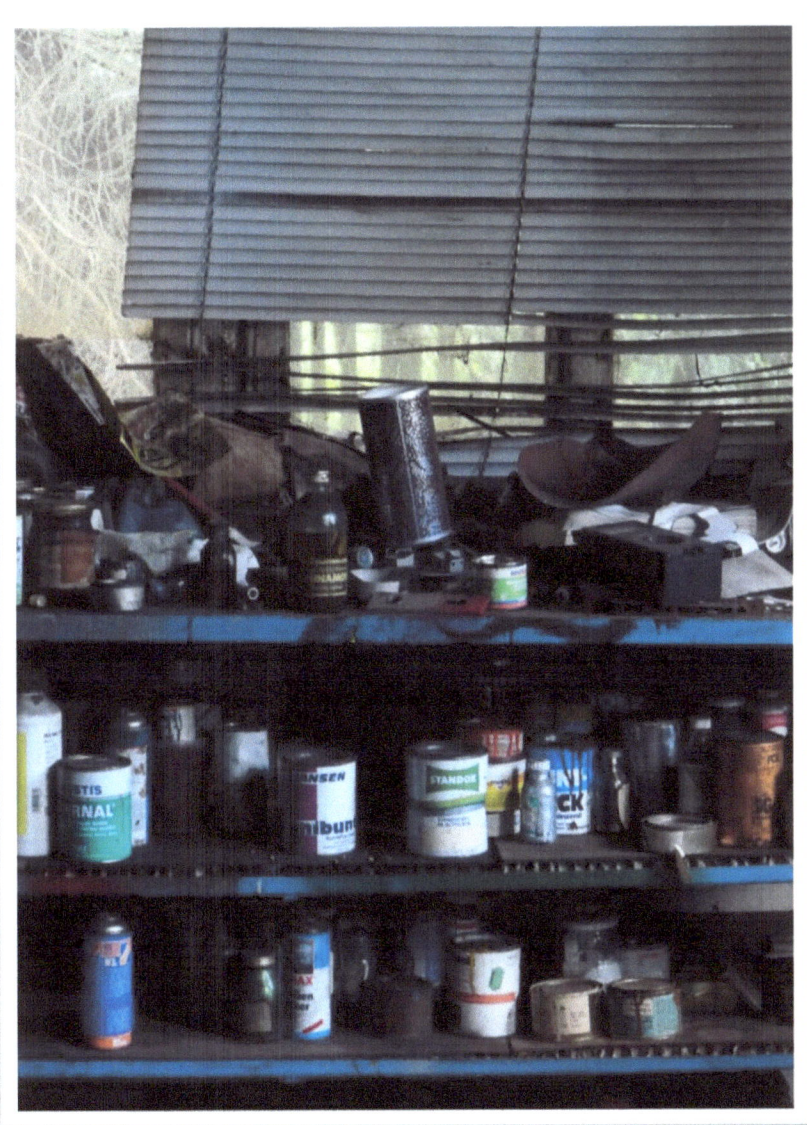

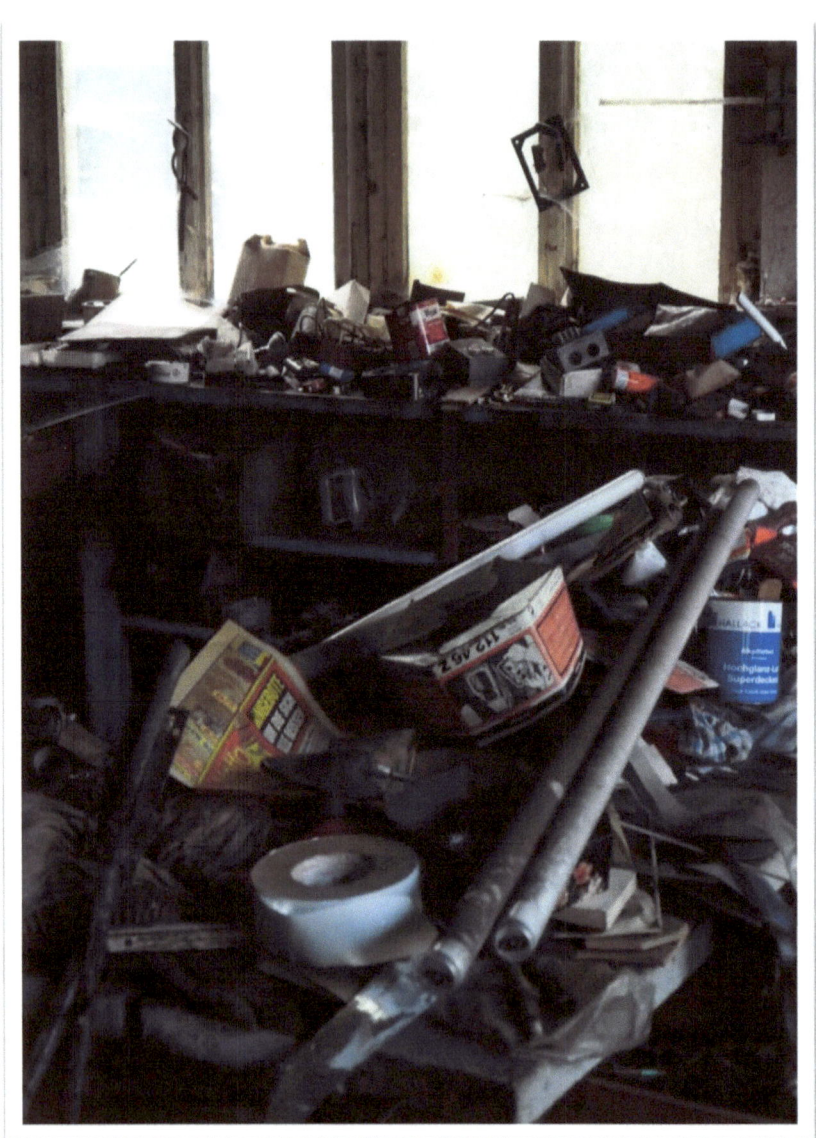

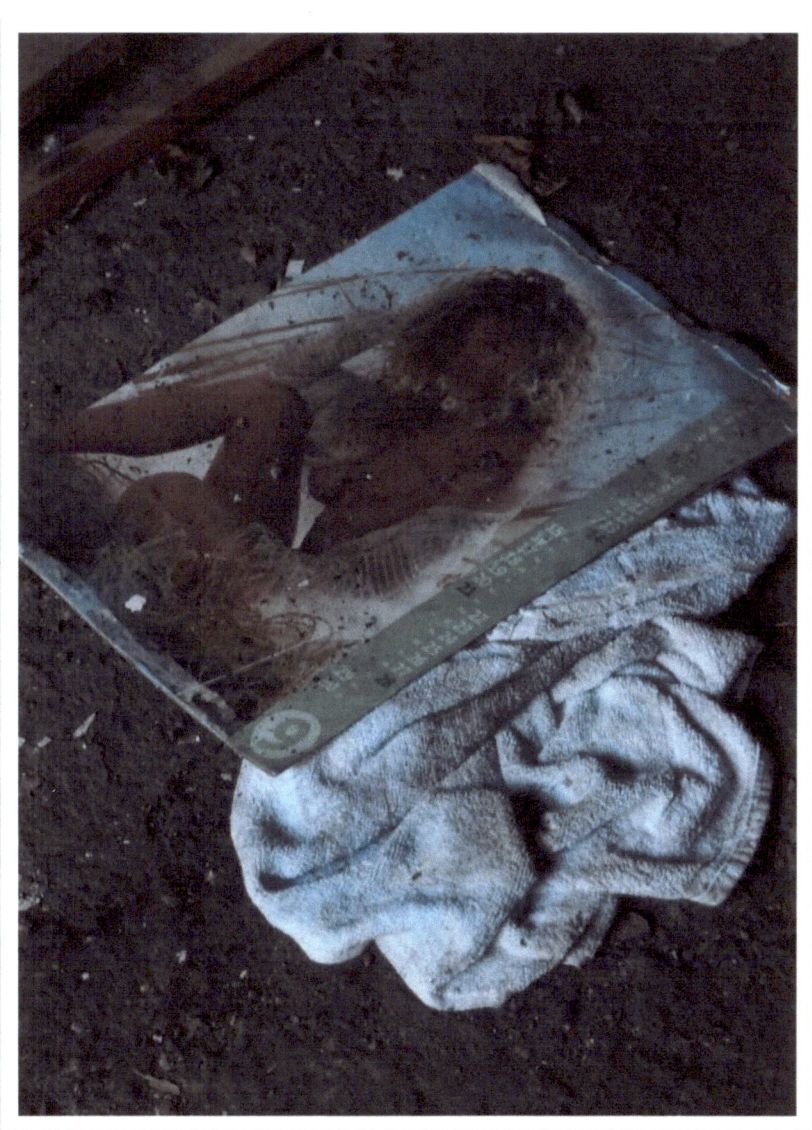

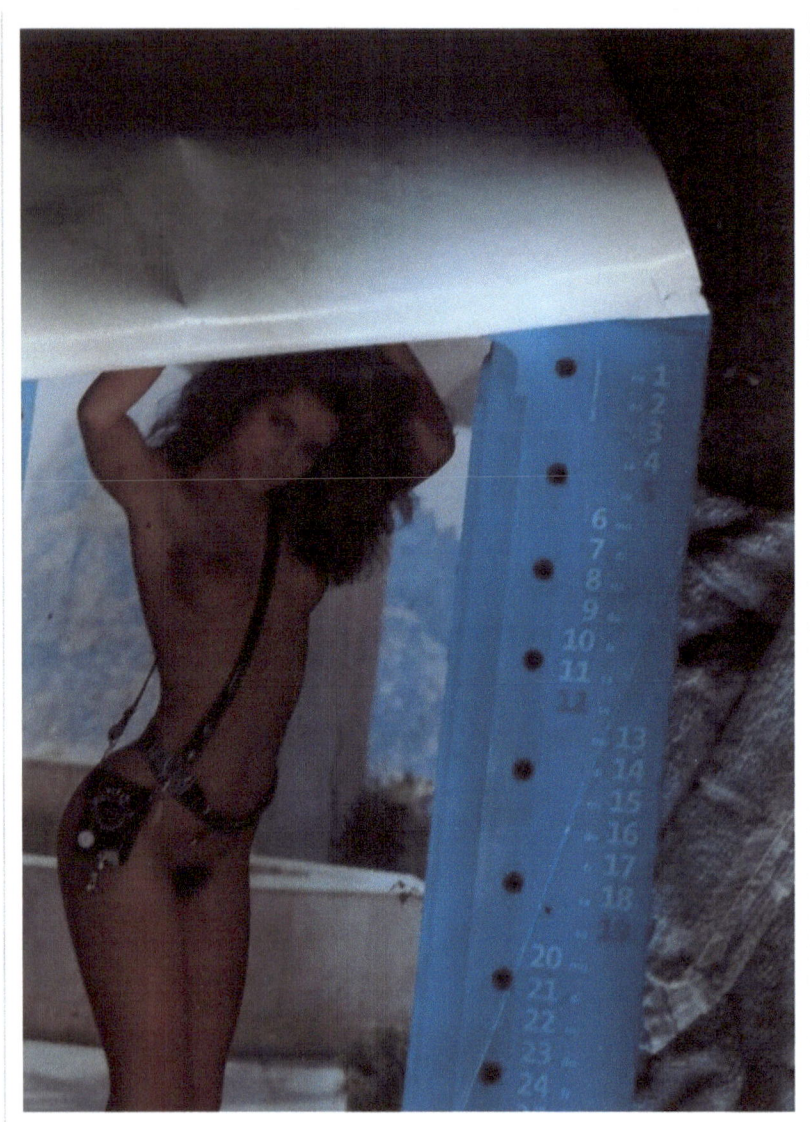

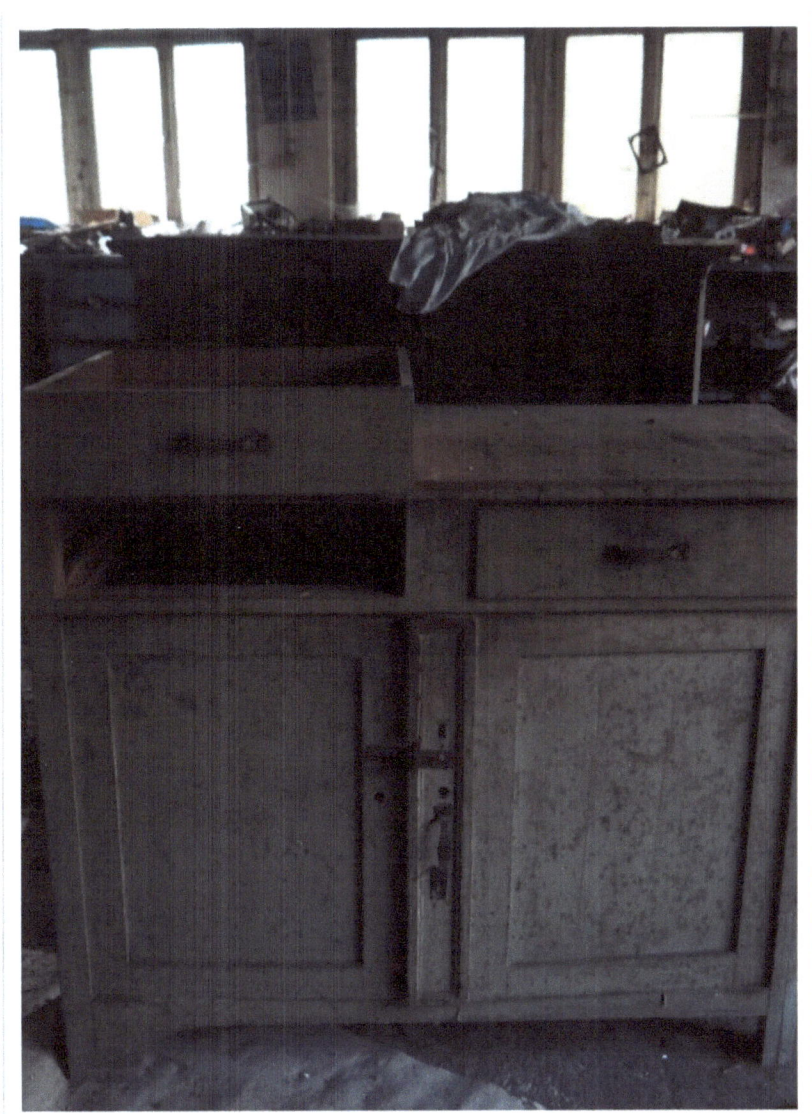

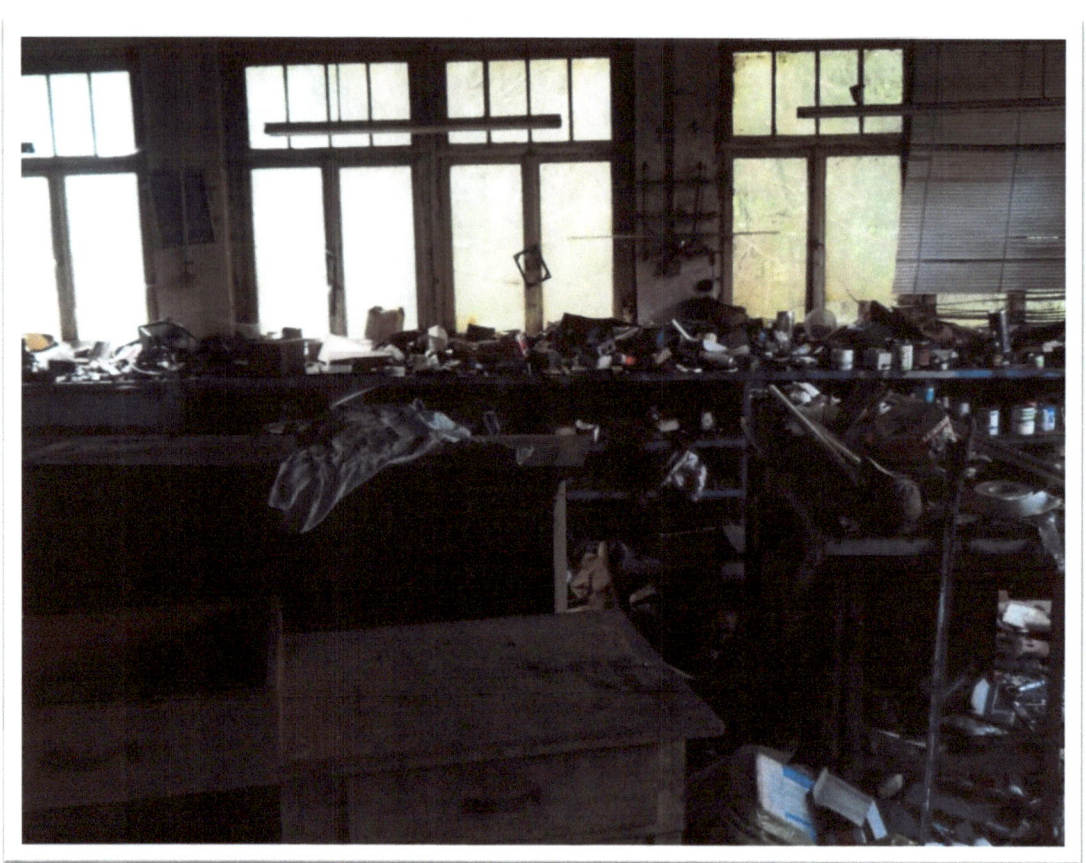

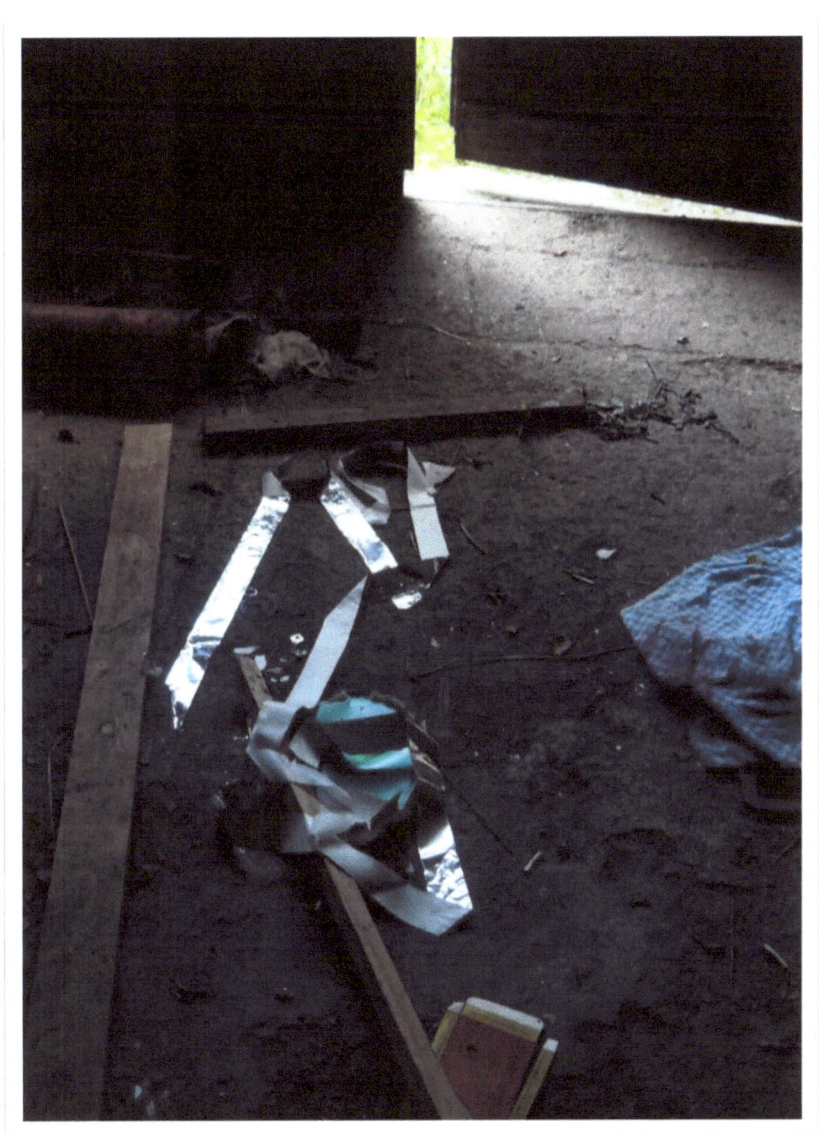

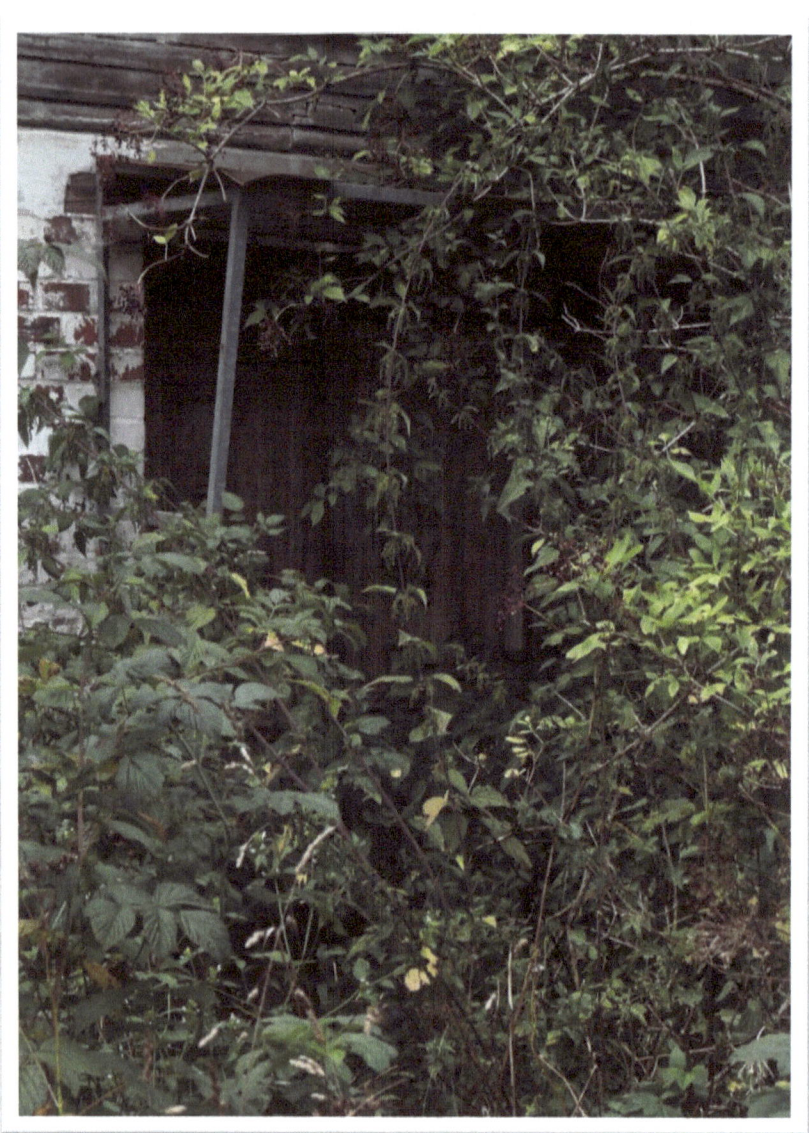

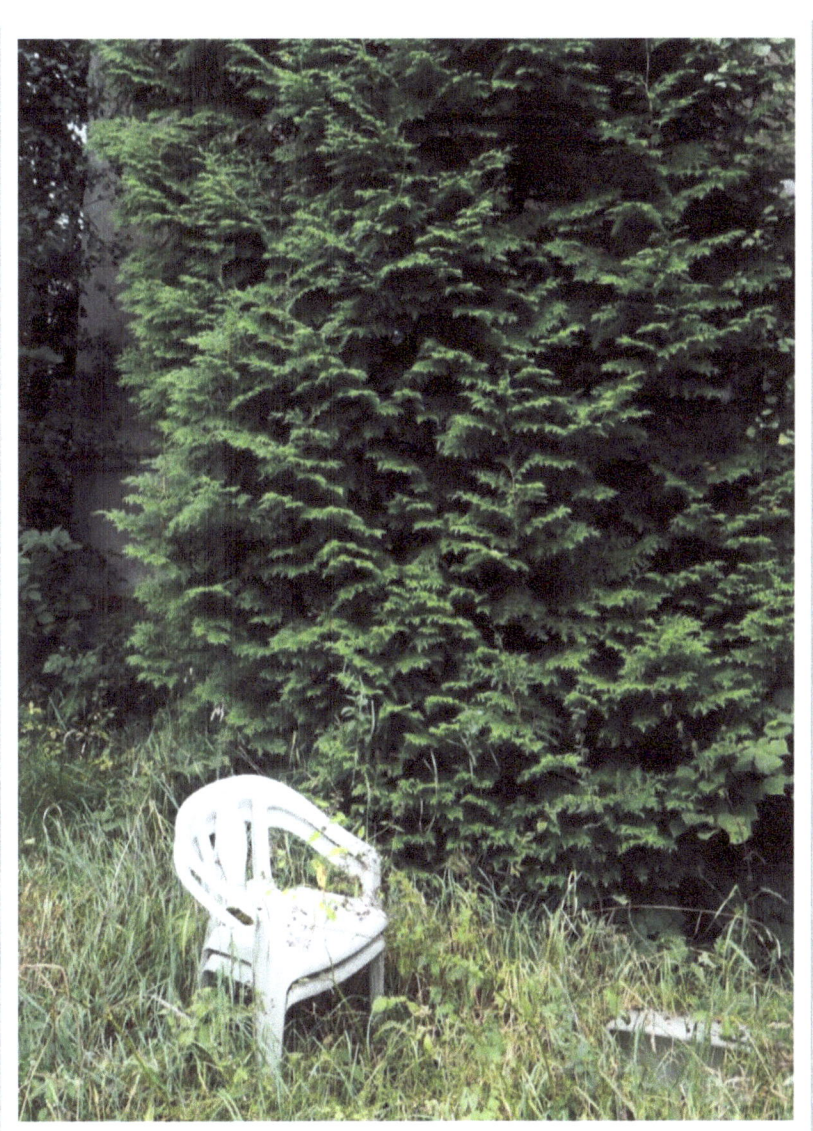

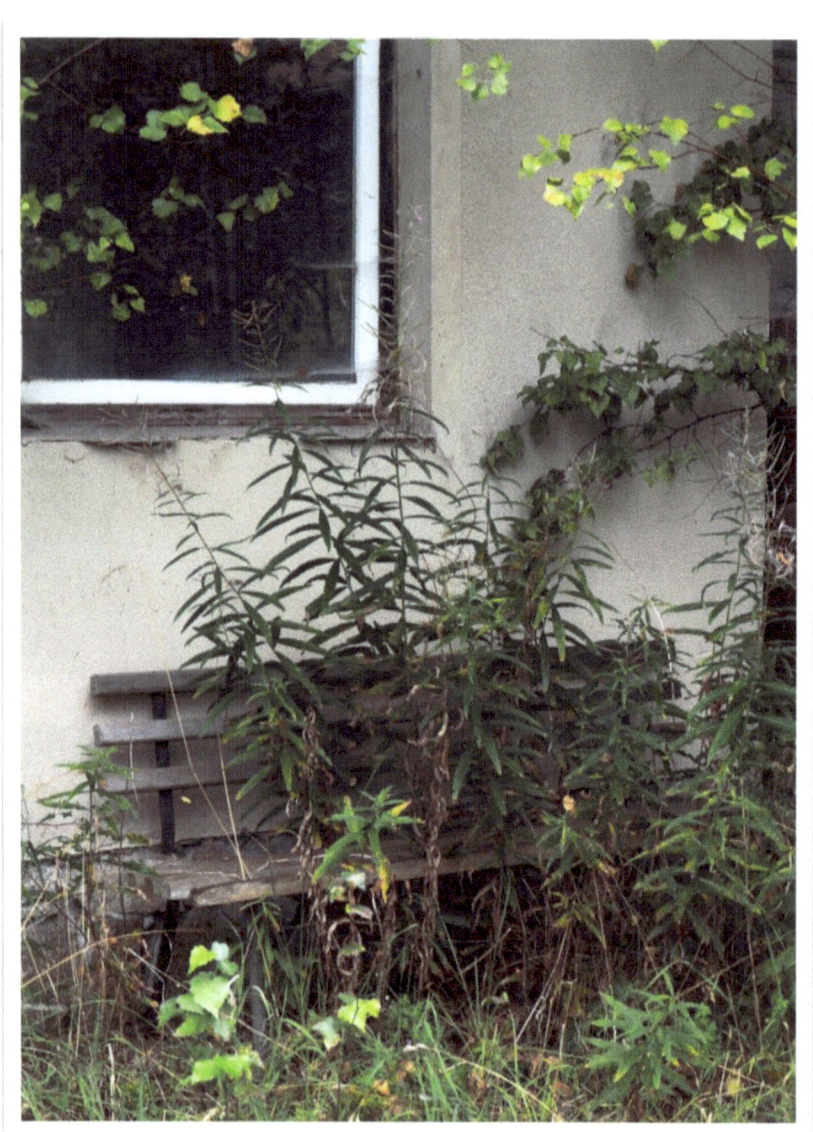

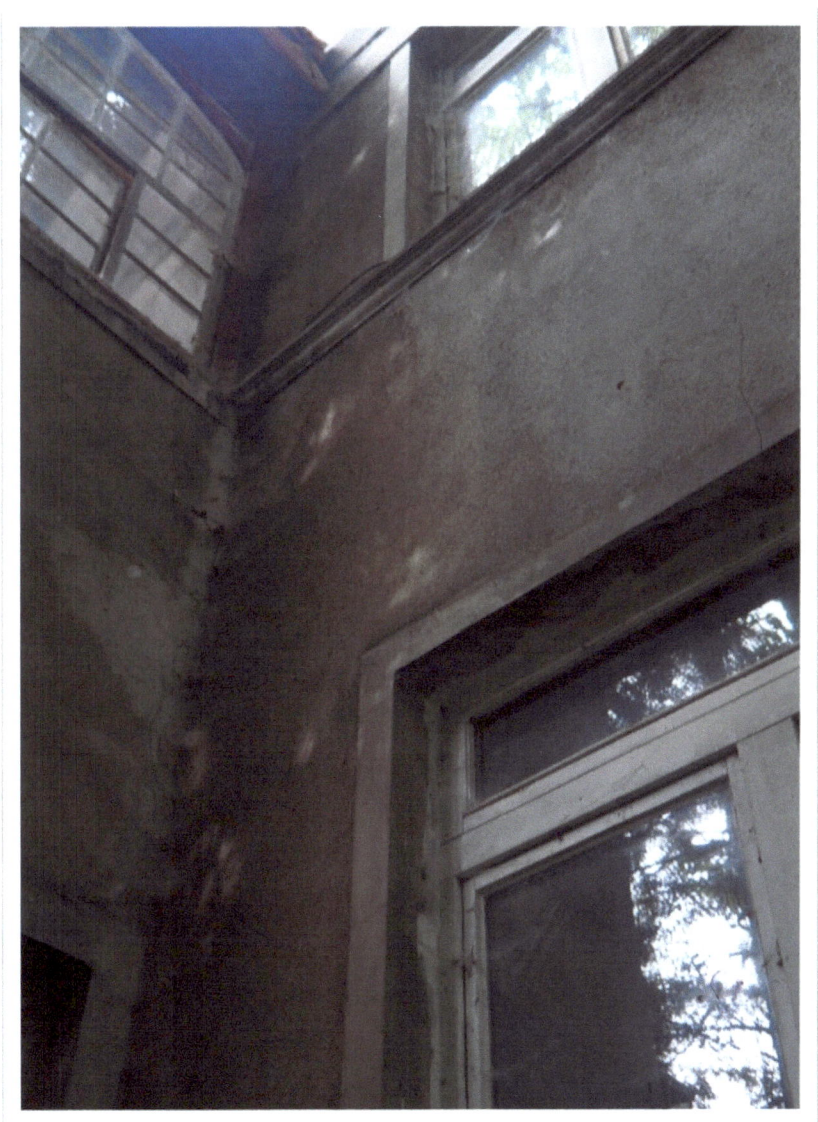

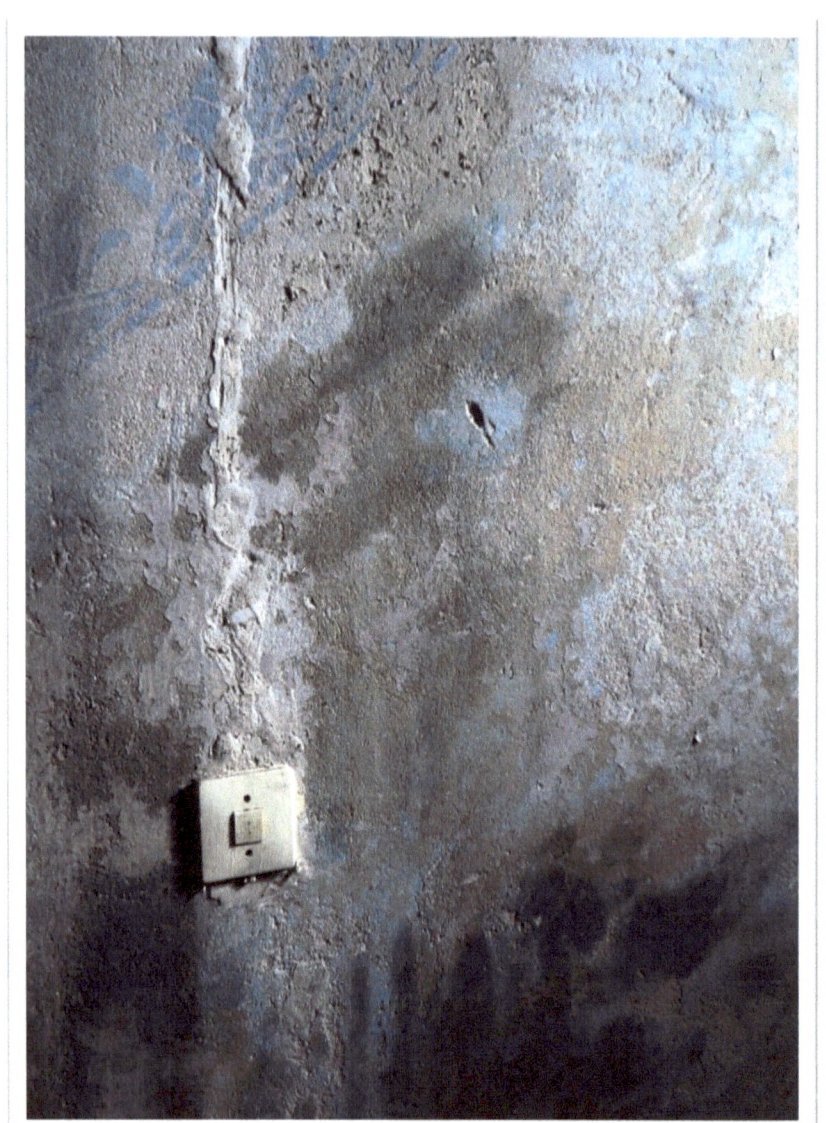

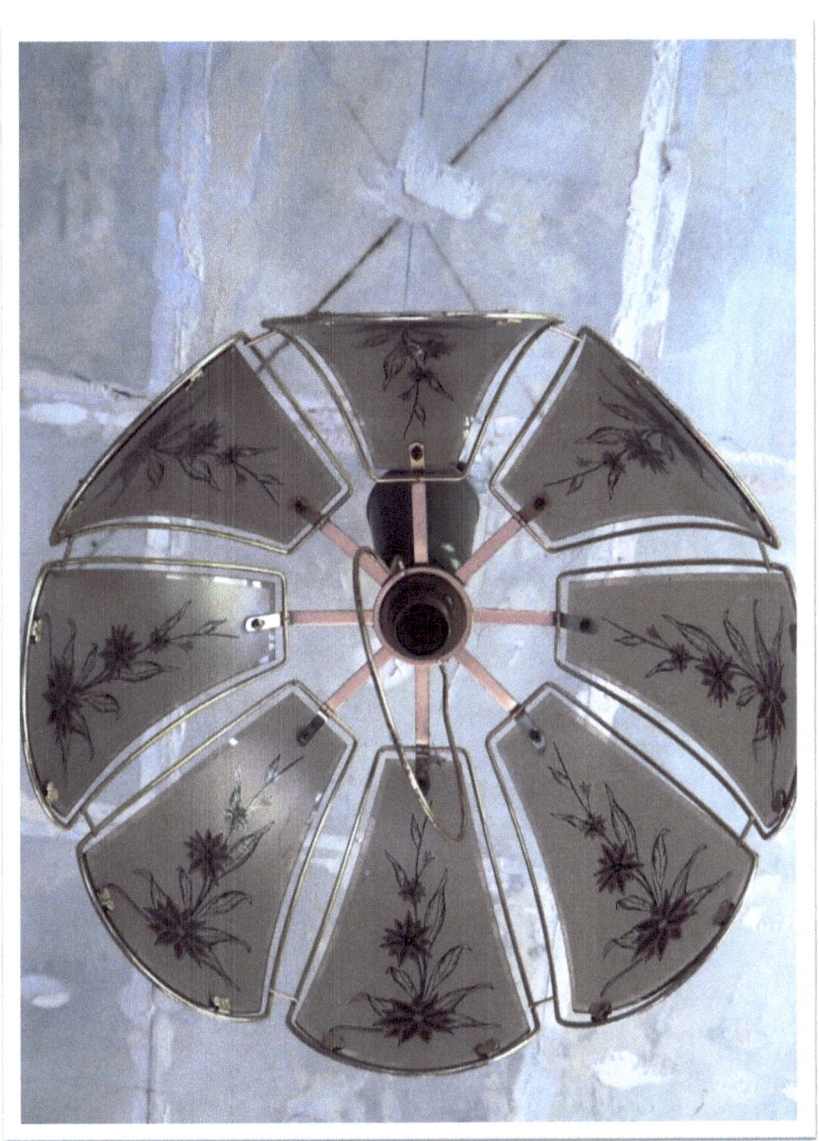

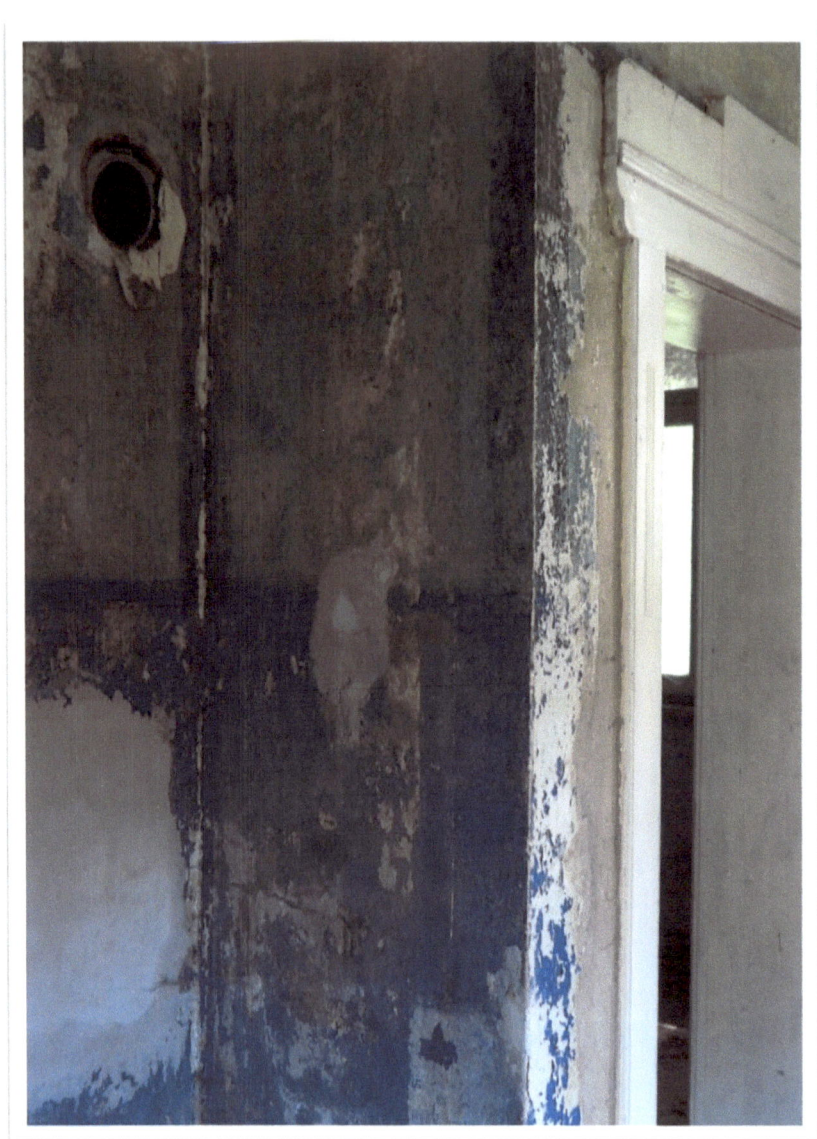

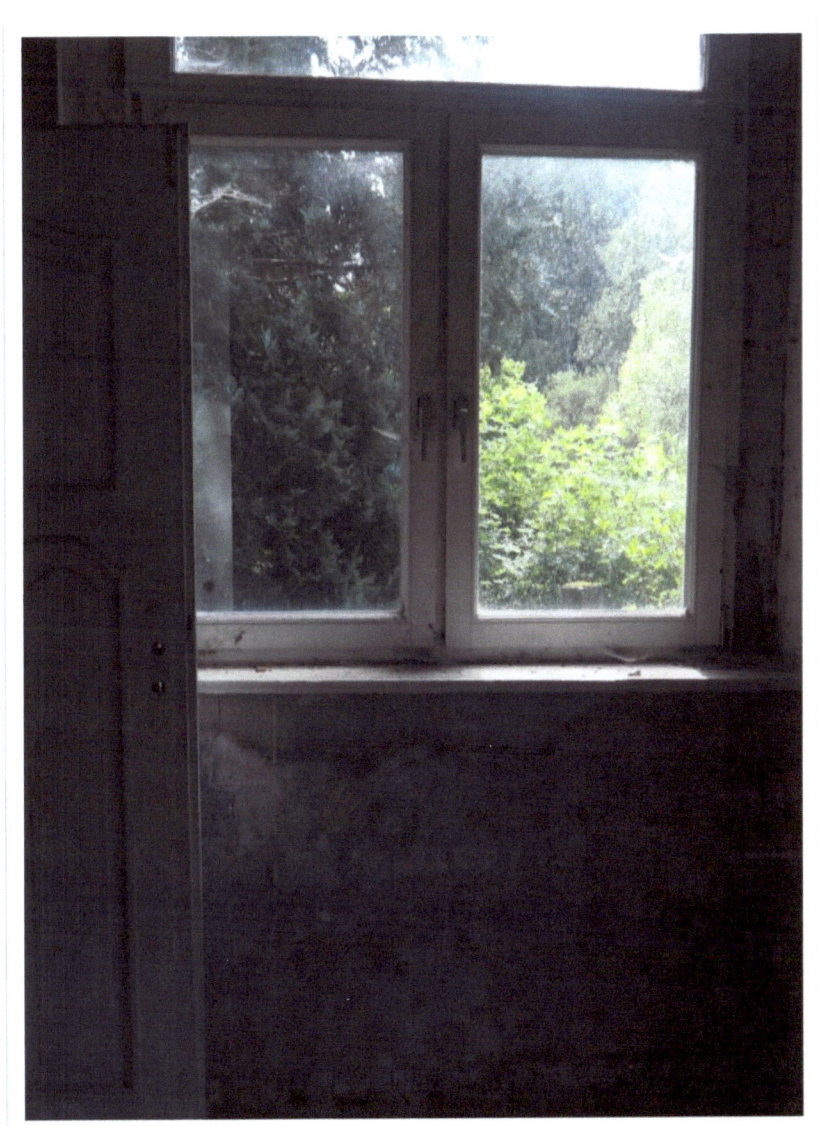

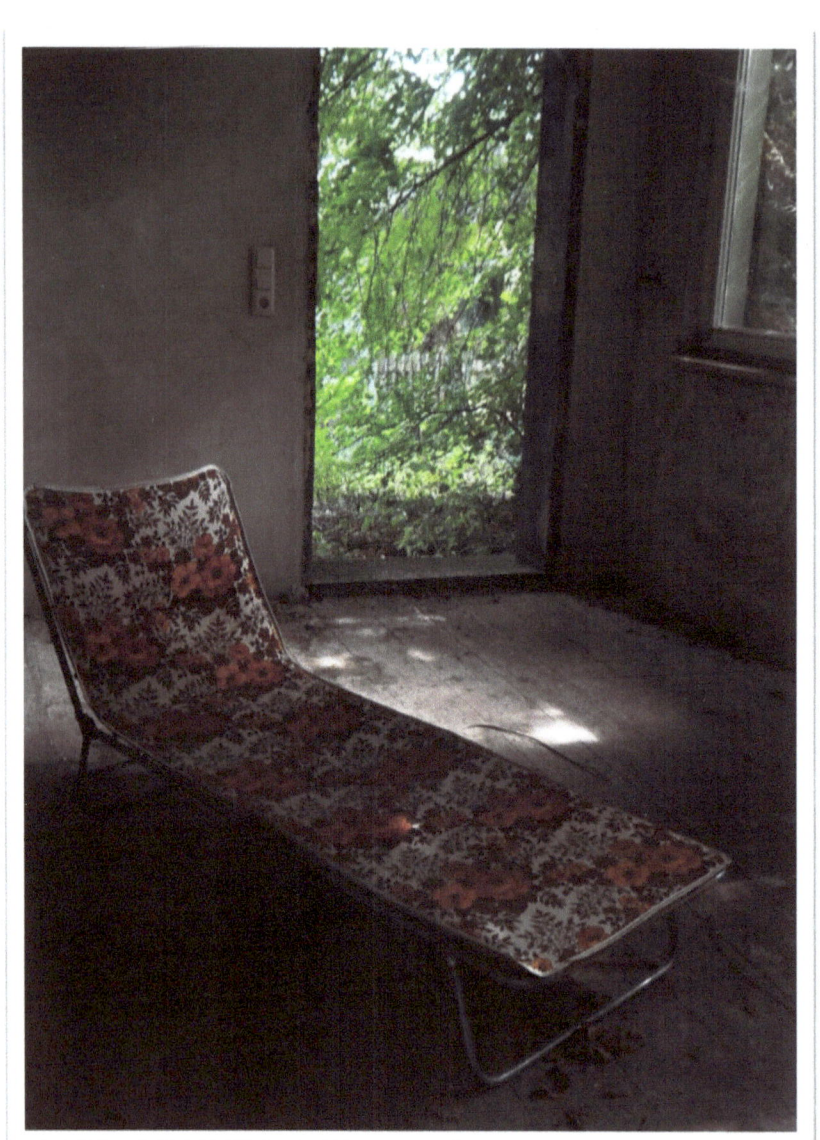

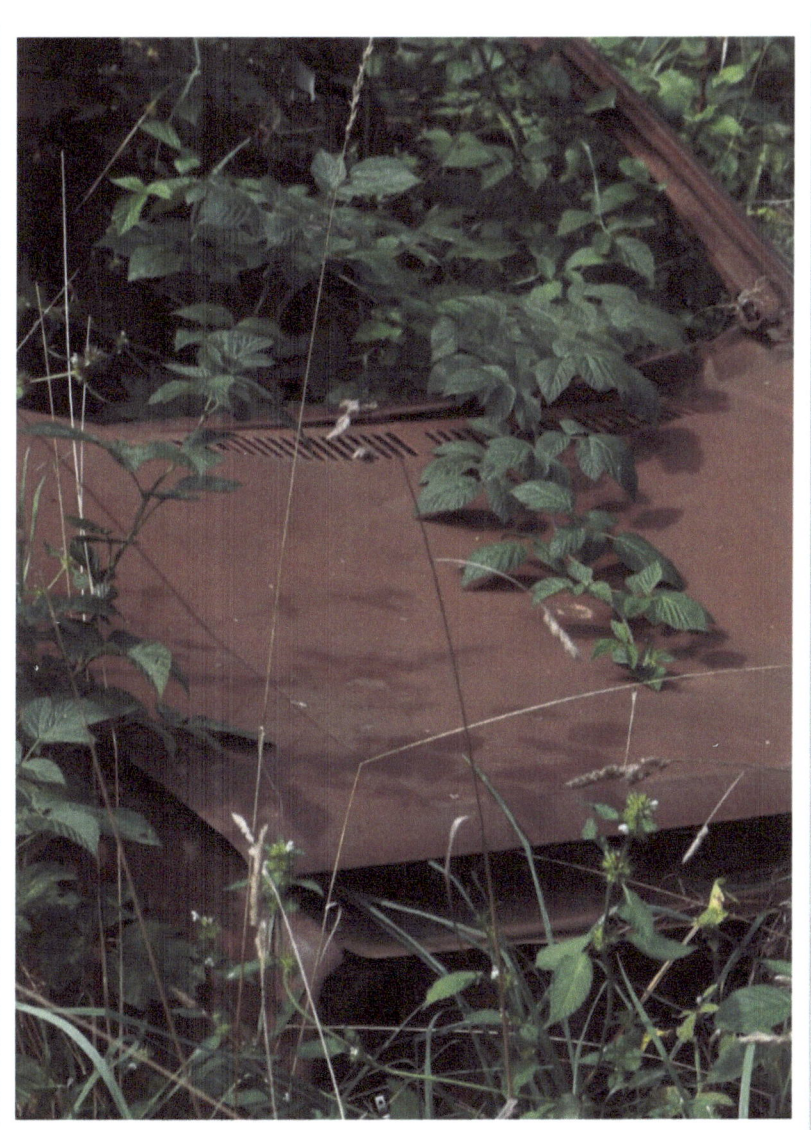

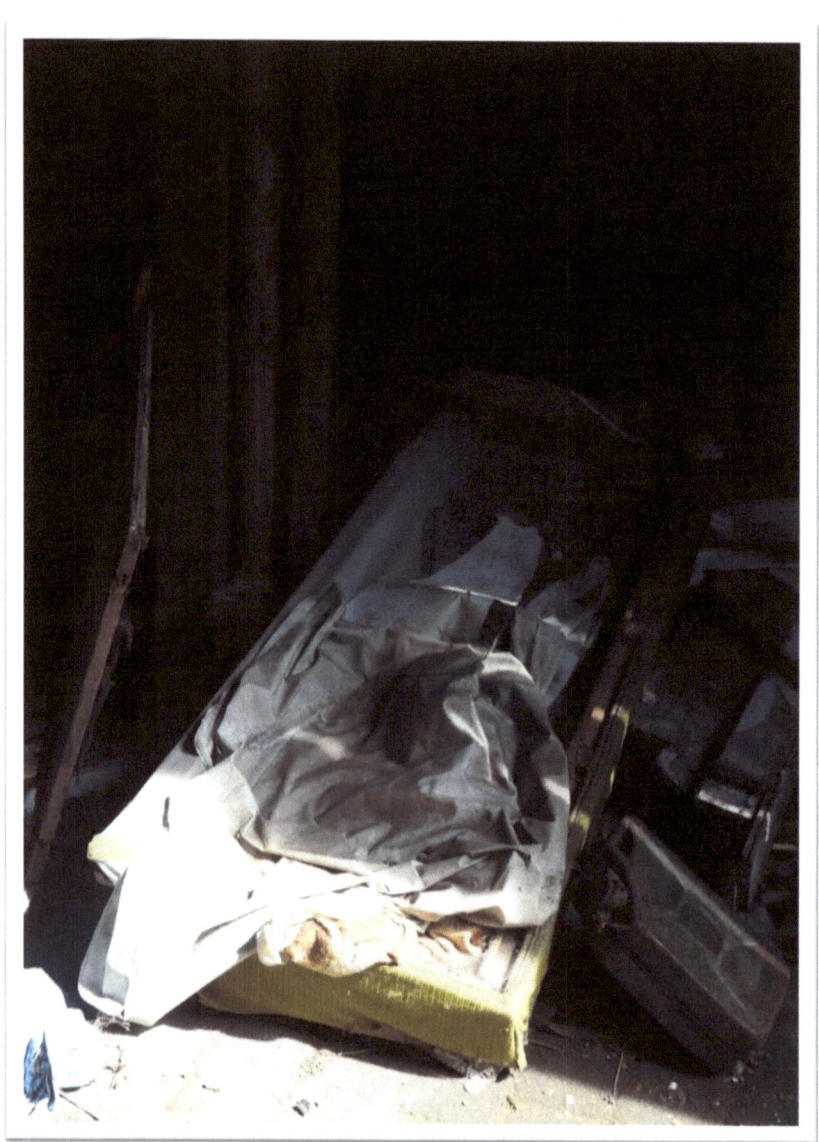

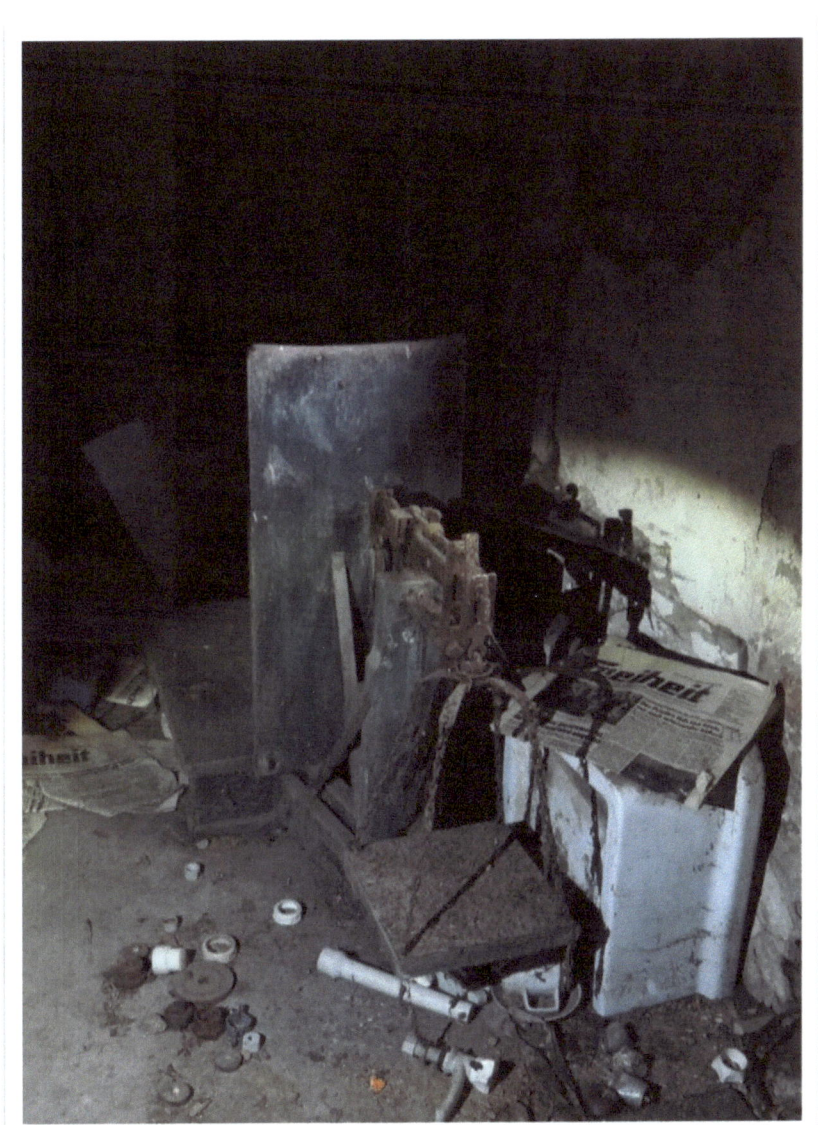

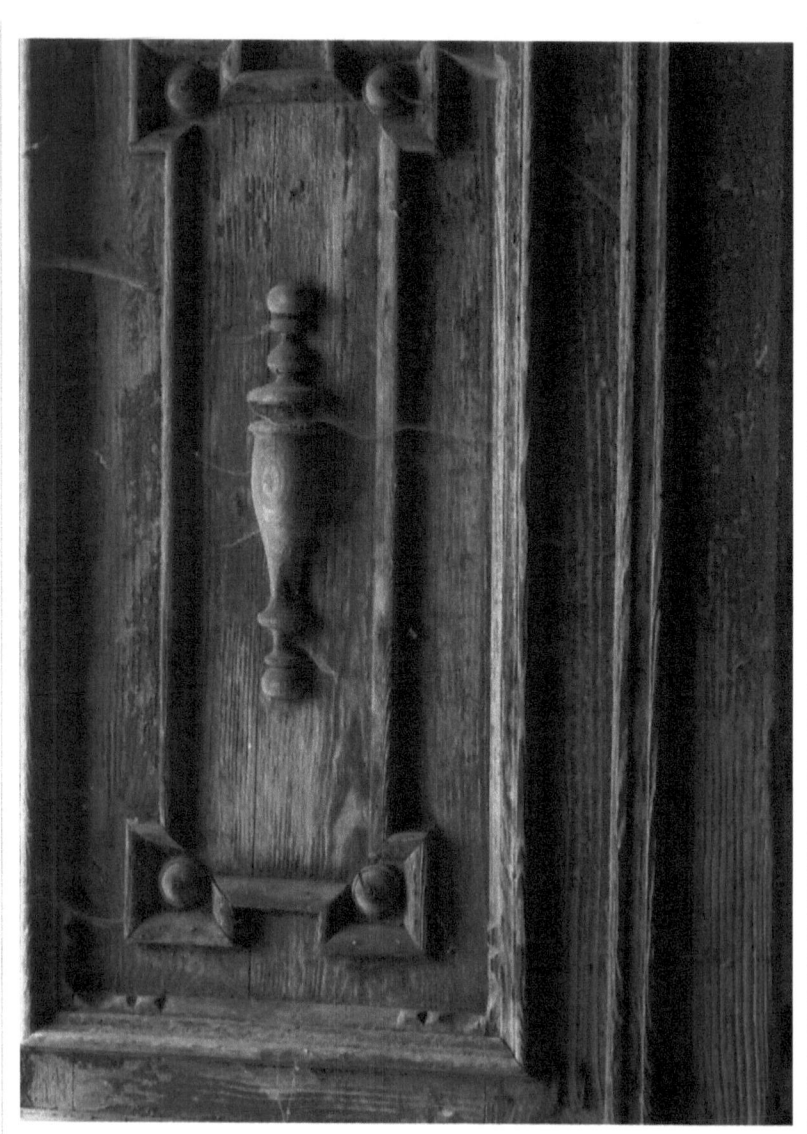

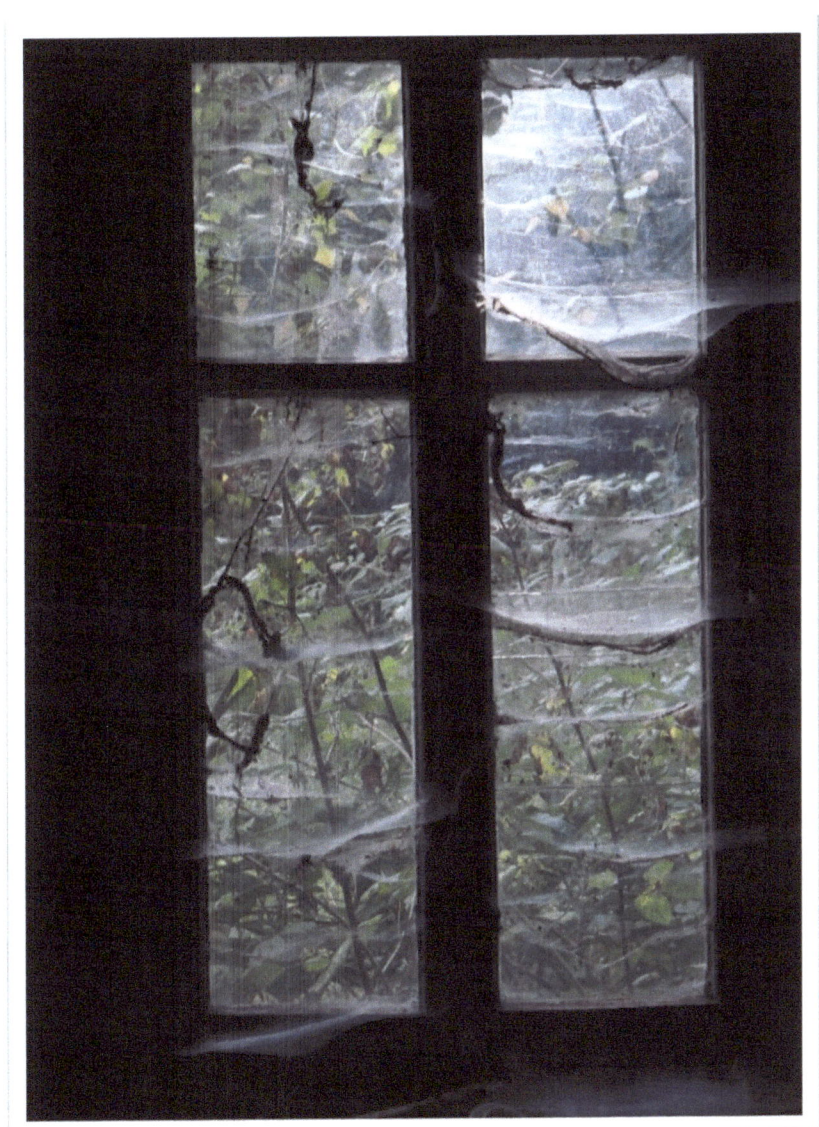

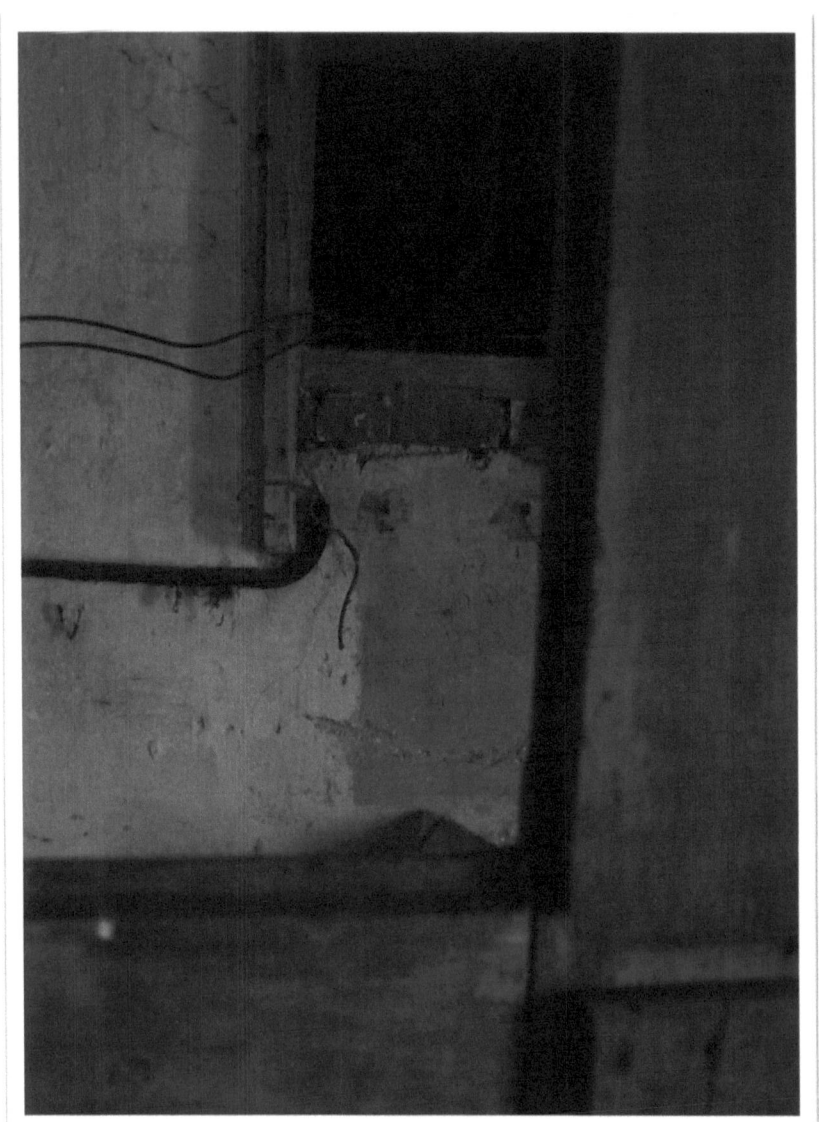

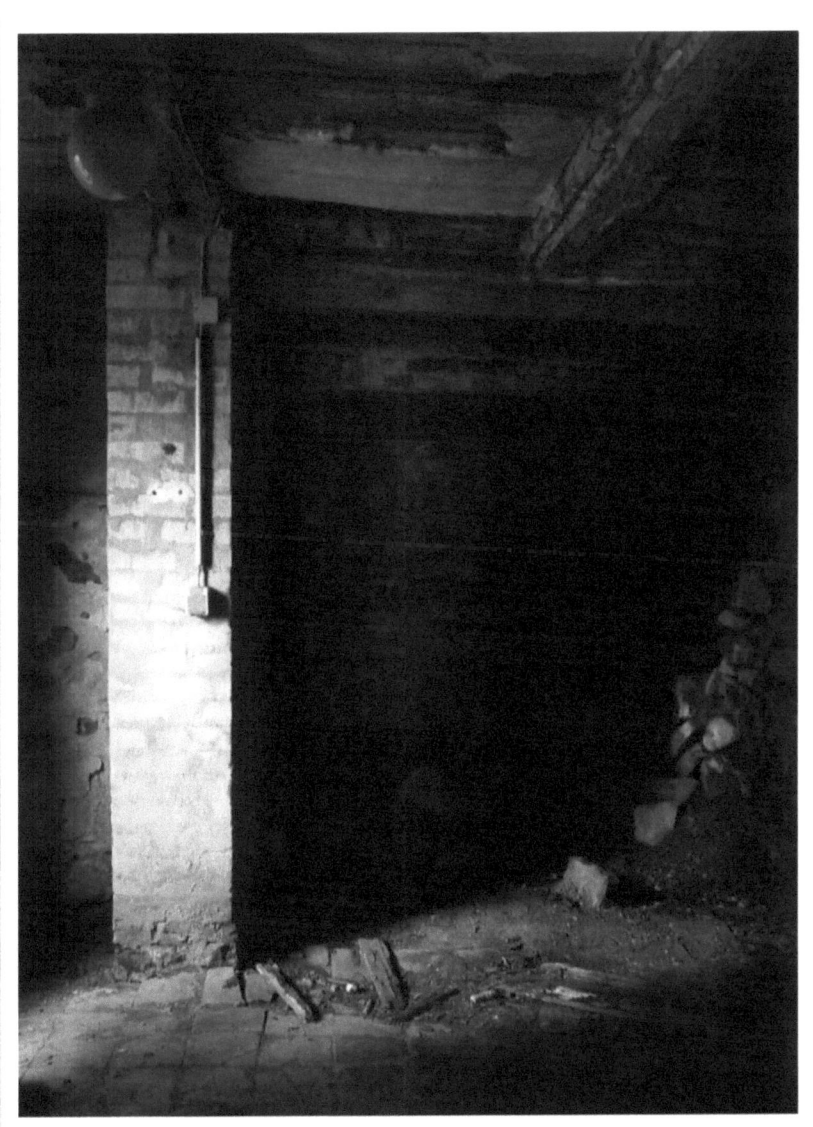

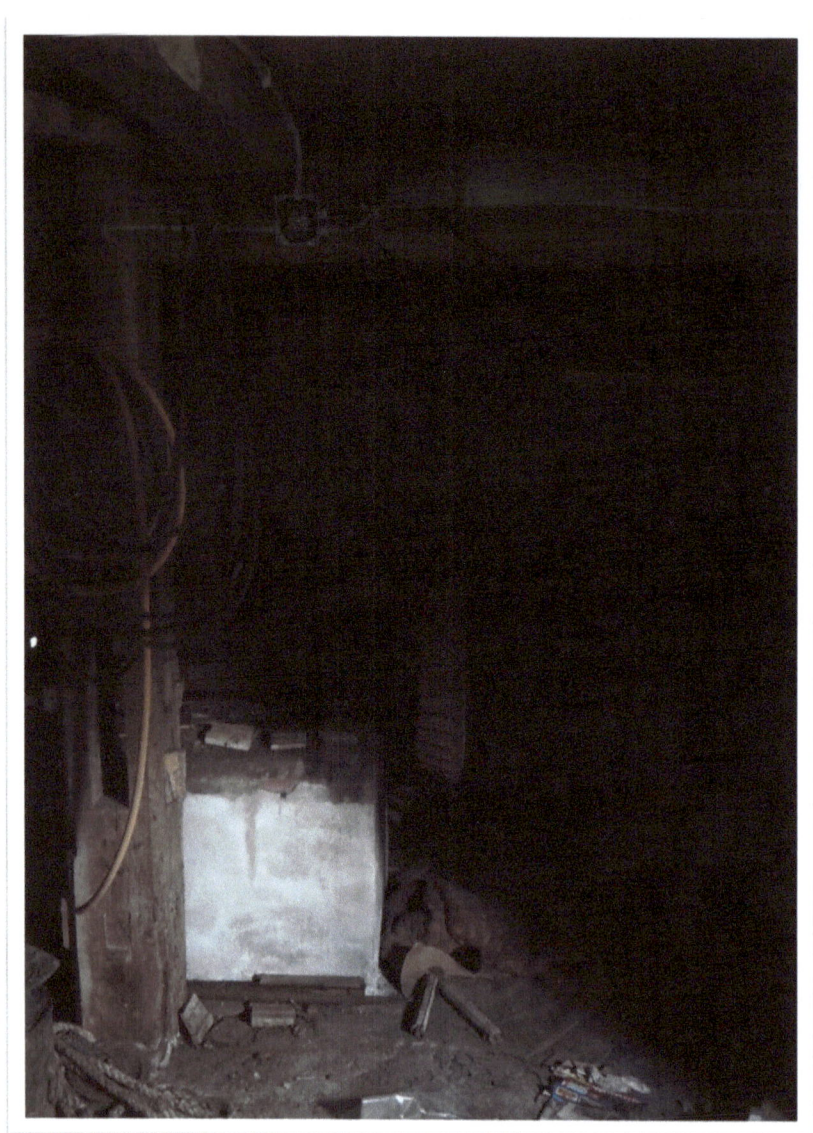

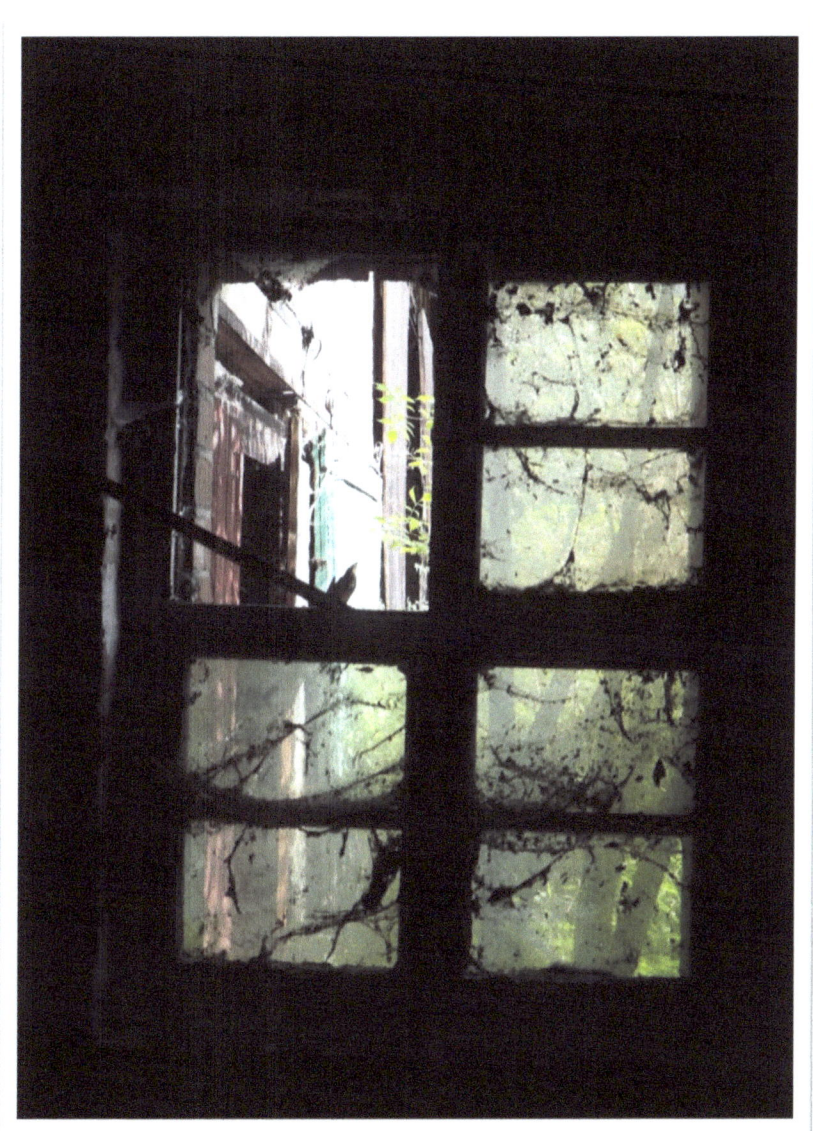

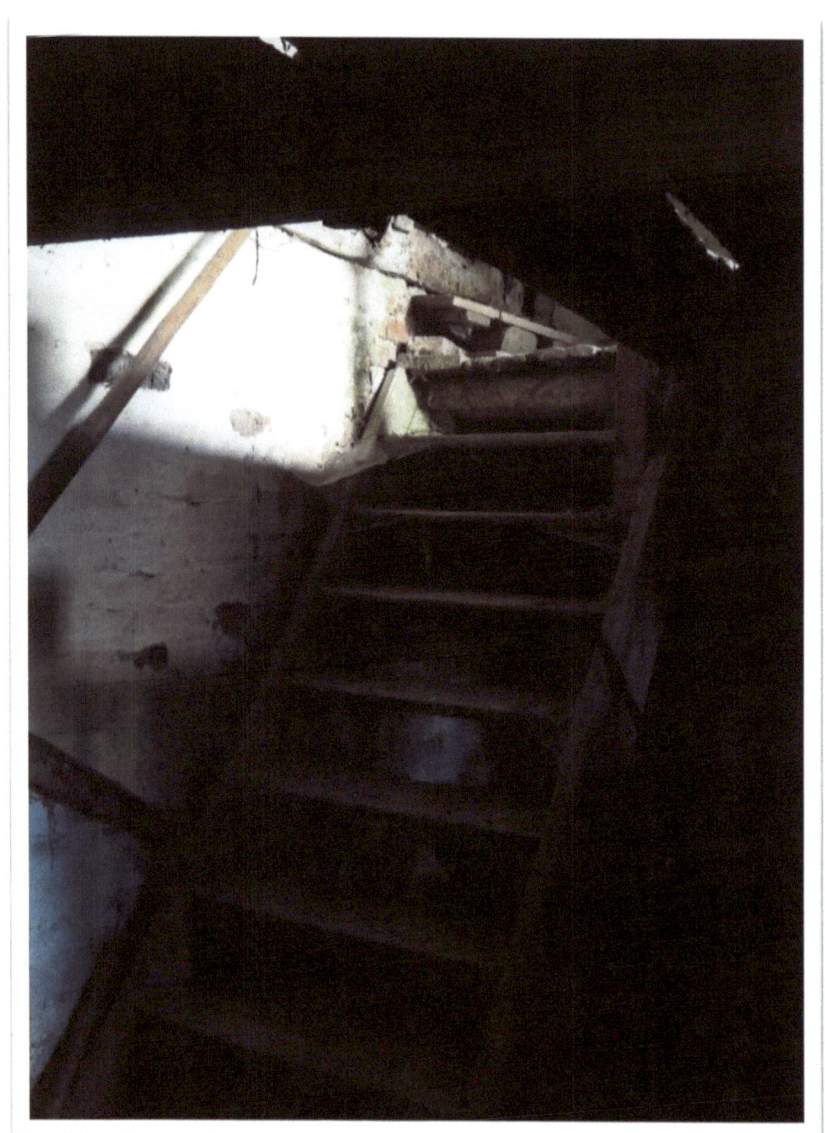

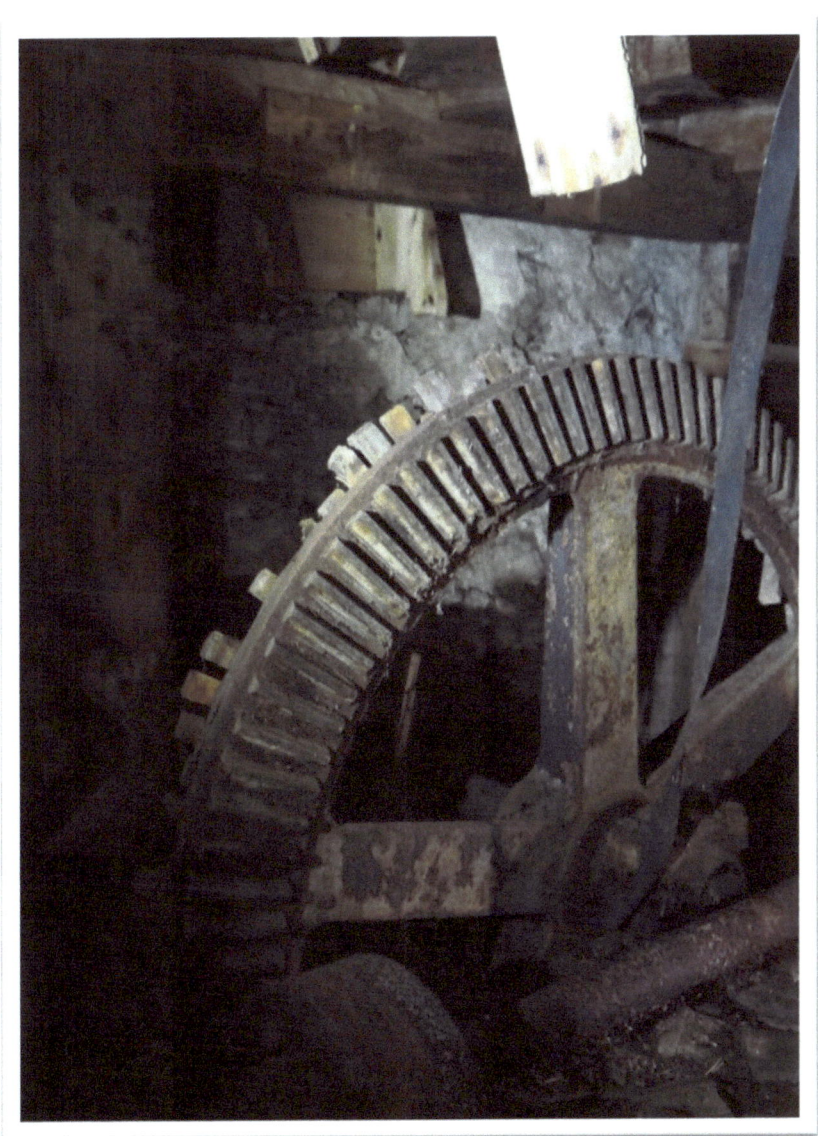

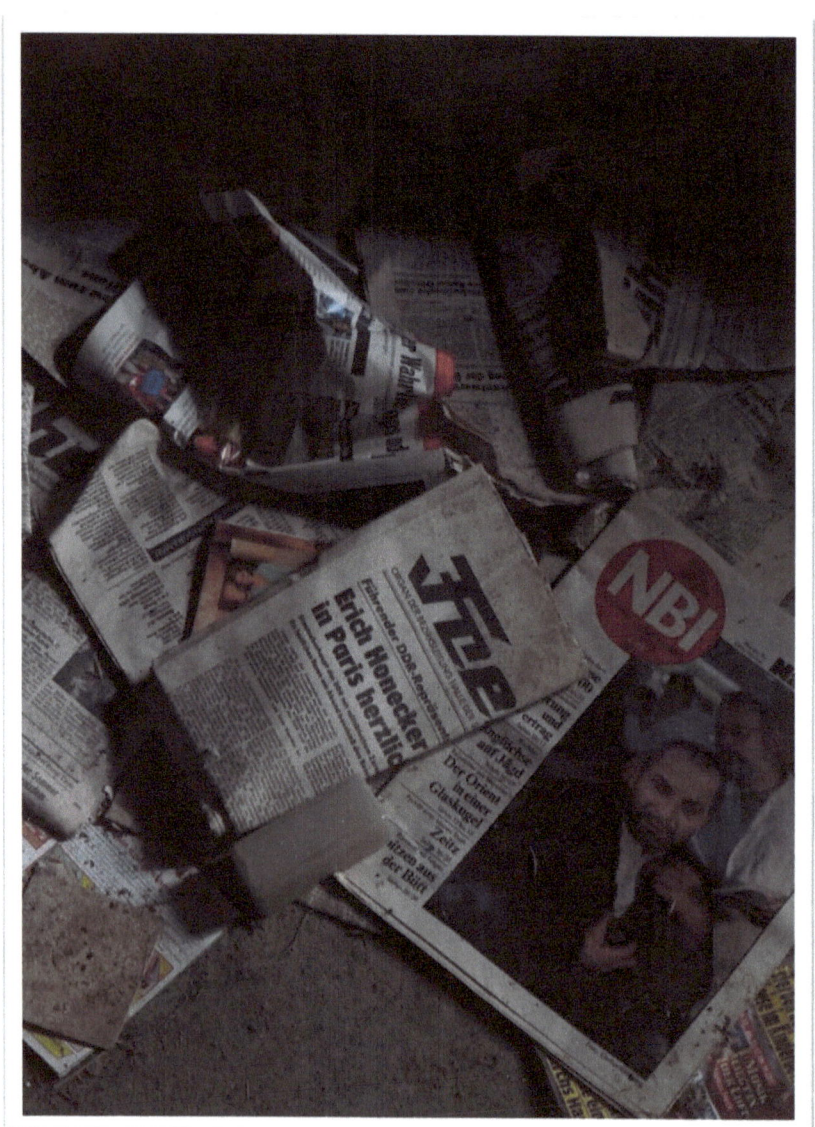

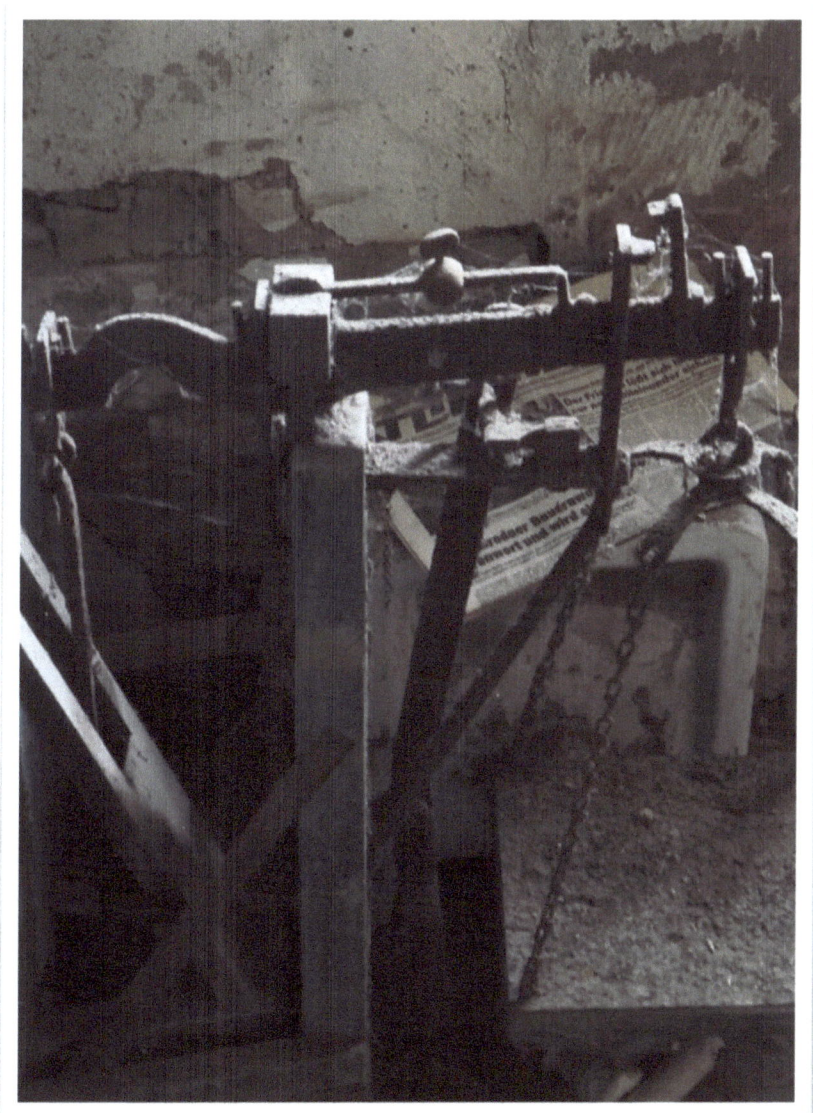

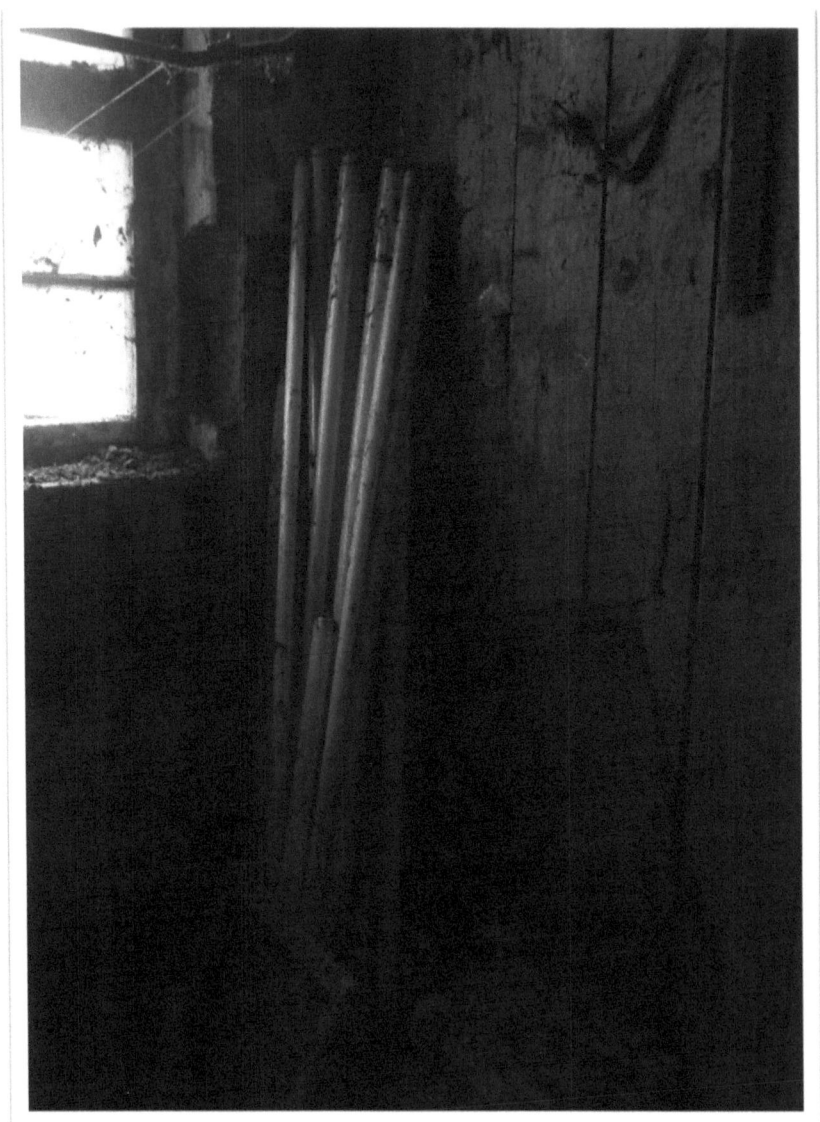

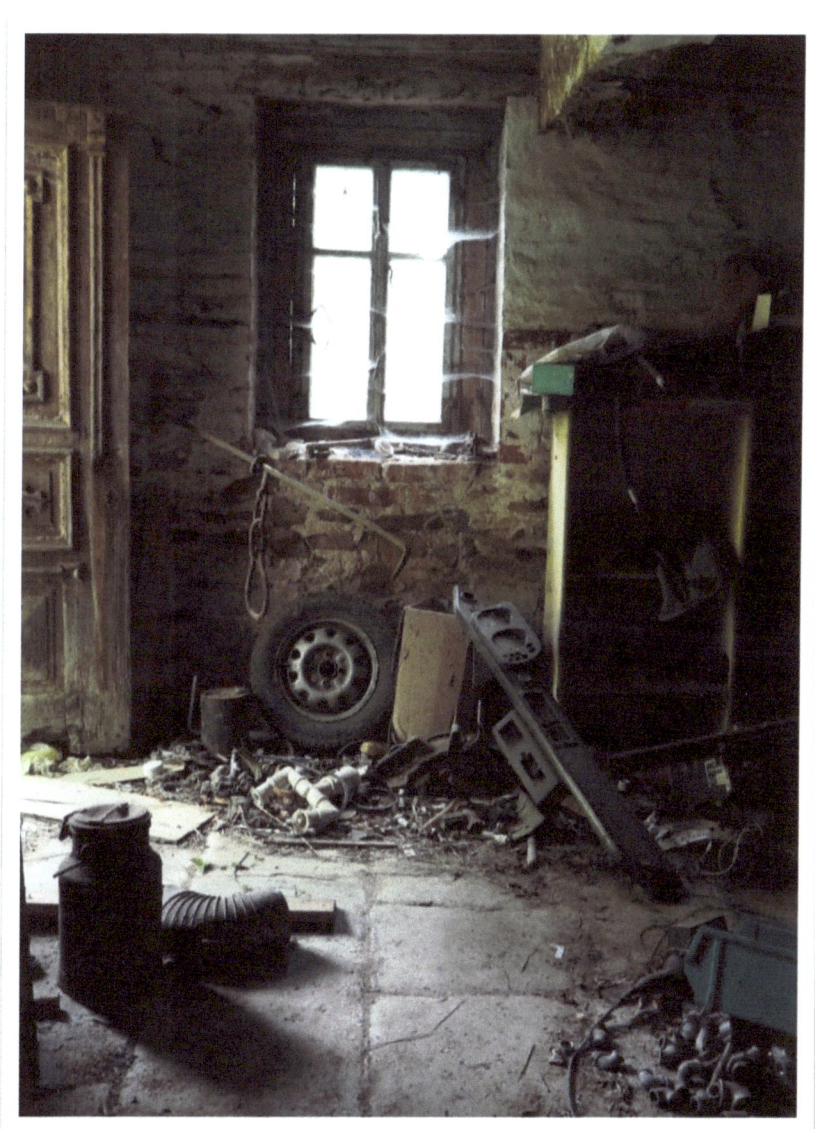

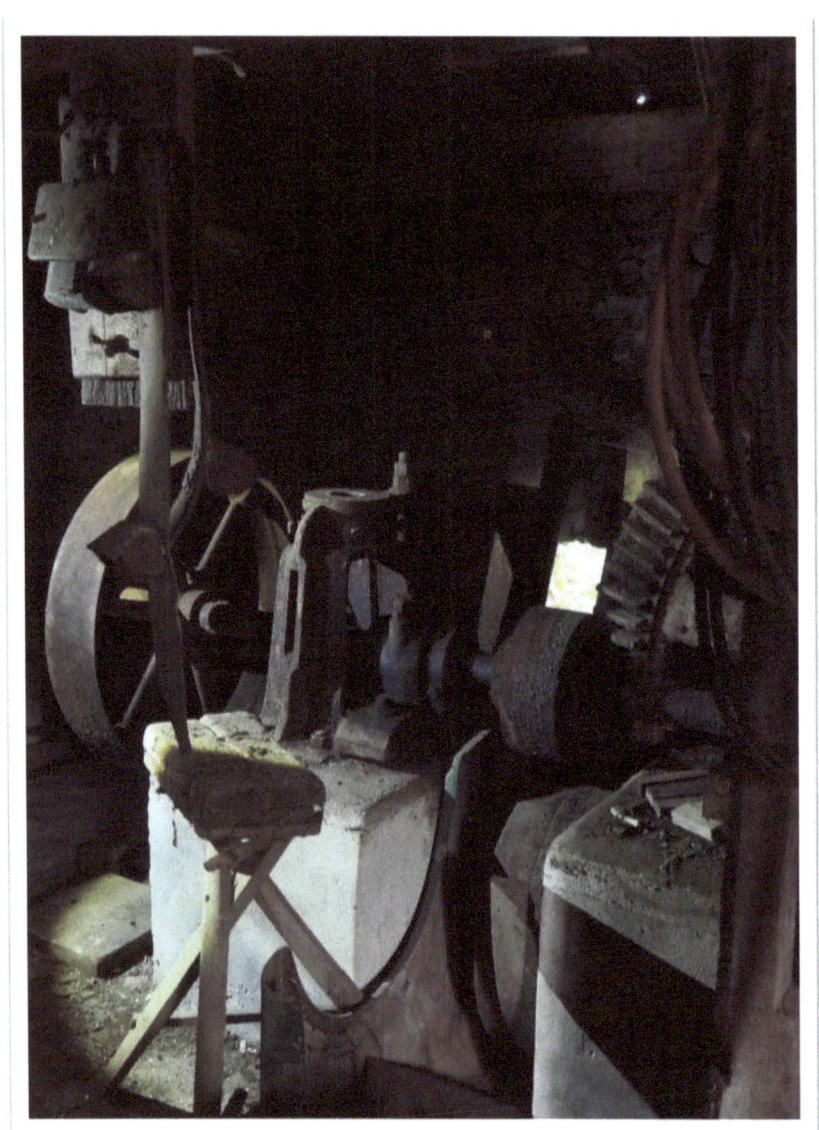

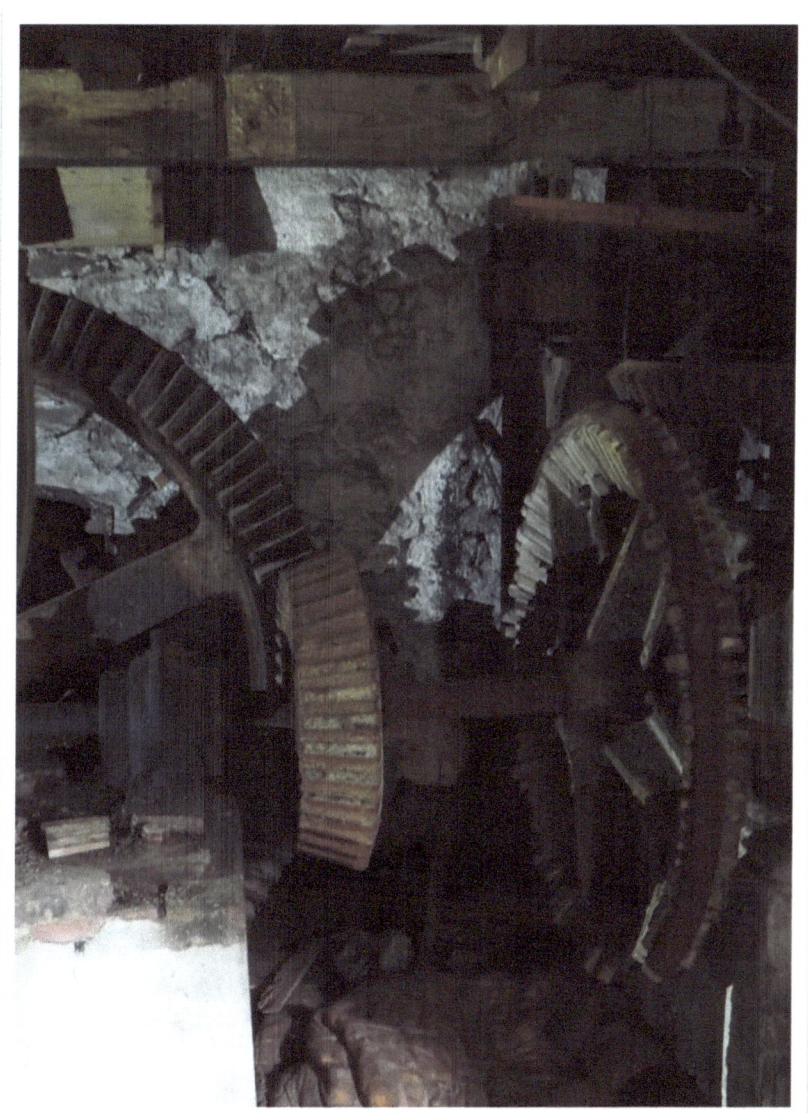

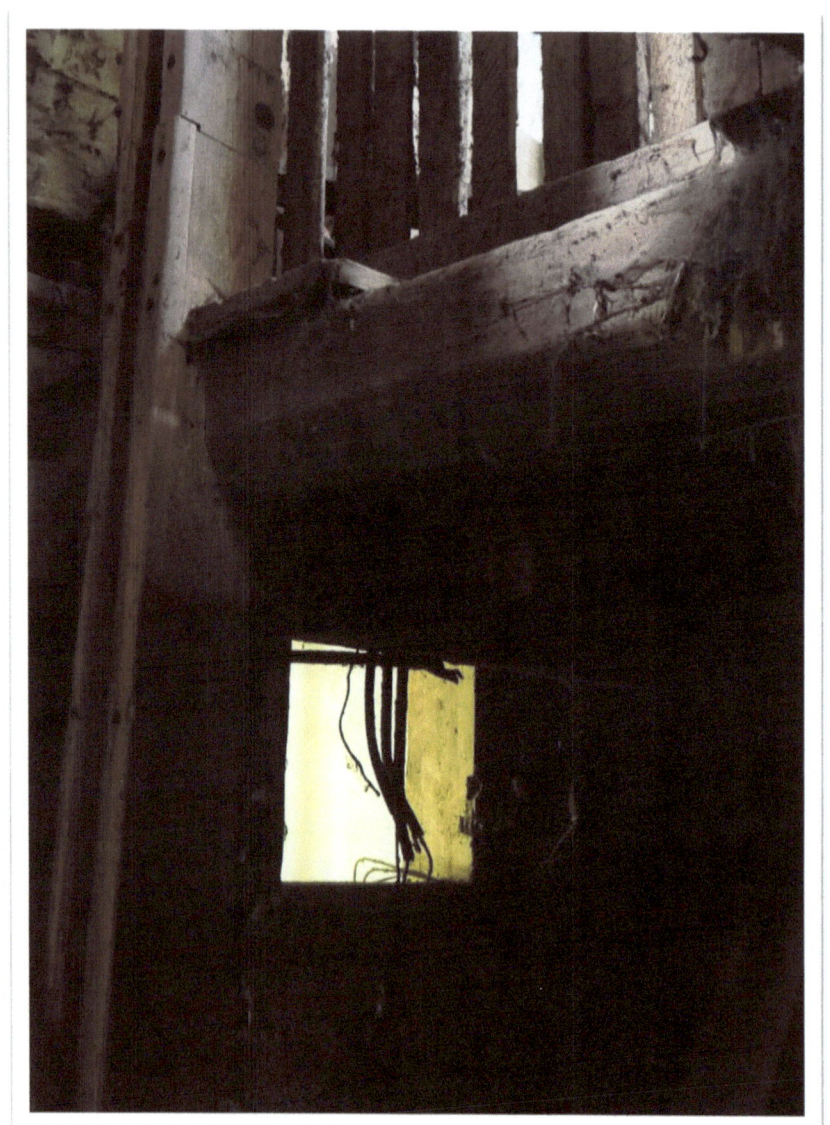

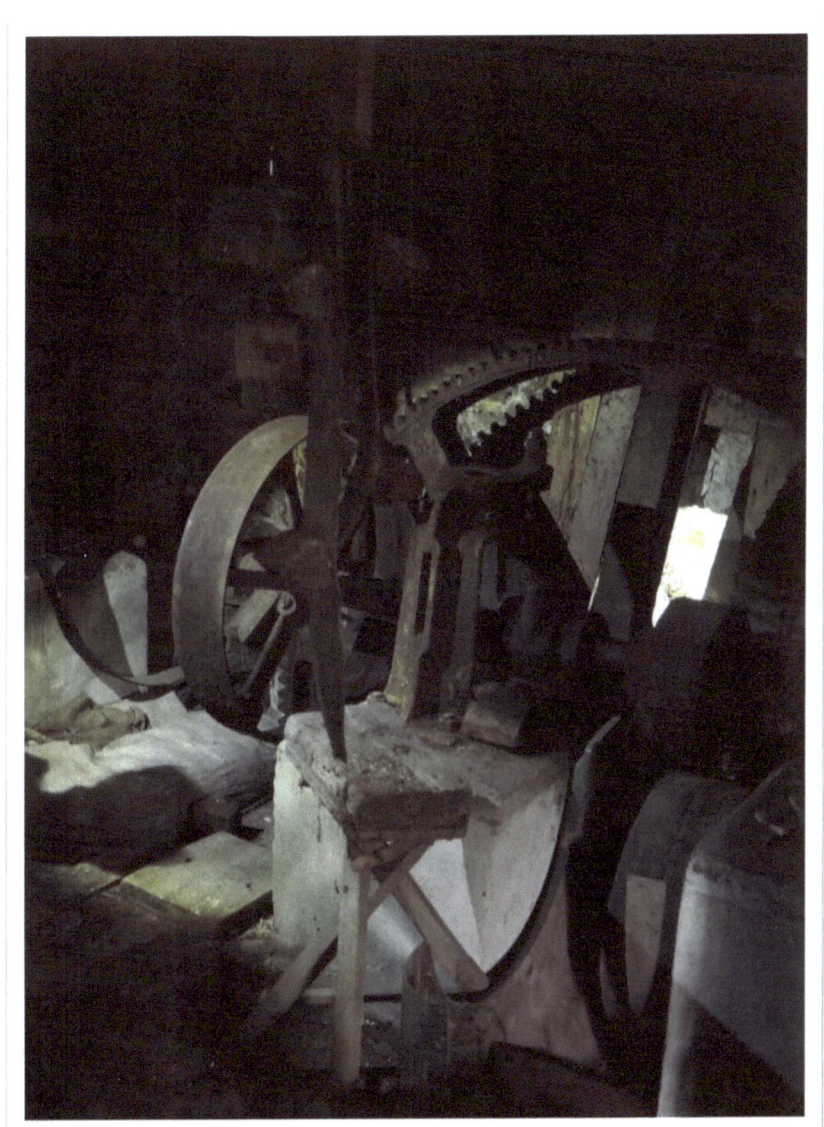